THE ROSARY: A GOSPEL PRAYER

Cover photo: high relief of Mother and Child by Ernest Morenon in Our Lady of the Rosary Chapel, National Shrine of the Immaculate Conception, Washington, D.C. Reproduced by permission.

THE ROSARY:

A Gospel

Prayer

W. J. HARRINGTON, O.P.

ALBA · HOUSE NEW · YORK

SOCIETY OF ST. PAUL, 2187 VICTORY BLVD., STATEN ISLAND, NEW YORK 10314

Imprimi potest: Flannan Hynes, O.P.
Provincial,
November 20, 1975

Library of Congress Catalog Card Number: 75-44676
ISBN 0-8189-1129-8

Designed, printed and bound in the United States of
America by the Fathers and Brothers of the
Society of St. Paul, 2187 Victory Boulevard,
Staten Island, New York 10314, as part of their
communications apostolate.

3 4 5 6 7 8 9 (Current Printing: first digit).

DEDICATION

In Memory
of
JOHN F. GLAZIER
who knew joy and sorrow and
lived in the hope of eternal glory

CONTENTS.

PREFACE.

The Rosary was never meant to be a mechanical repetition of the Hail Mary, punctuated by the Our Father and the Glory. It was always meant to be a meditative prayer. It is intended to be a meditation on the mysteries of our redemption revealed in the Scriptures. Properly understood, the Rosary is not the prayer of the unlettered — though anyone can pray it. And it is not a pathetic relic of the past. That is, unless one is prepared to discard the Gospel on which the Rosary is firmly grounded.

That firm Gospel basis is the concern of this book. It is not my intention to propose any method, let alone a new method, of praying the Rosary. It is not my object to up-date the Rosary. What I have set out to do is to study the New Testament ground of the Rosary. In its modest way, this is a work of exegesis and biblical theology. I have striven to be positive and I have desired to be helpful. The Rosary cannot be properly prayed without the use of the Scriptures, even if that use is implicit. So much the better if we have a good understanding of the Scriptures. A professional exegete might be expected to make his contribution.

I realize that my presentation would be more aesthetically pleasing if the treatment of the Fifteen Mysteries were uniform. This was, in fact, a thought that did occur at the planning stage. In practice, such a procedure proved unfeasible. This is a Bible-oriented study and had to be guided by the biblical data. The Joyful Mysteries are based on the first two chapters of Luke — while the Sorrowful Mysteries look to the lengthy passion-narratives of all four gospels. And there is, obviously, more to be said about the Resurrection than about the Visitation. The mysteries of the Rosary are revelatory. It is wise to follow the pattern of revelation in Christ.

I am indebted to the scholars listed in what is, after all, a very select bibliography. I am especially beholden to Fr. Raymond E. Brown. From him, and not only from his great commentary on the Fourth Gospel which is chiefly in question here, I have learned much. I am very thankful to my friend Michael Glazier who suggested this book, and to Fr. Francis X. Borrano, SSP, who undertook to publish it. Its appearance is quite due to them.

W.J.H.

INTRODUCTION.

The Rosary is a thoroughly biblical, a wholly Gospel prayer. The reason it is so is by no means only because the Lord's Prayer and the greater part of the Hail Mary, come straight from the gospels. It is because almost all the 'mysteries' of the Rosary come straight from the gospels. The Joyful Mysteries àre taken from the first two chapters of Luke, his infancy gospel; the Sorrowful Mysteries are based on the passion narratives of the four gospels; and the Glorious Mysteries reflect the close of the gospel and its overflow into the new age of the Spirit and the Church.

Like many familiar words, the term 'mystery' can, when used in certain contexts, be confusing. In common parlance, 'mystery' means secret, hidden, not readily discernible — we speak of a detective-mystery. The older catechism defined mystery as revealed truth which we cannot comprehend. Perhaps the mysteries of the Rosary have something of both meanings. But I believe that we are on the right lines when we turn to the New Testament. The later Pauline writings speak of the 'mystery' long kept secret by God but now 'made manifest to his saints' (Col. 1:26). It emerges that the mystery is identified with the person of Jesus Christ (Eph. 3:4; Col. 4:3; 1 Tim. 3:16) and, at the same time, is identical with the Gospel: the proclamation of the Gospel *is* the mystery which was kept secret for long ages (Rom. 16:25). We learn that for Mark, too, while the content of the mystery is the kingdom of God (Mk. 1:14f; 4:11), the presence of the kingdom in the person of Jesus – the 'mystery' which he proclaims – is 'the word' (4:33), that is, the Gospel. Indeed, Mark can clearly identify Jesus with the Gospel (8:35; 10:29). The mystery which has been given to the disciples involves above all an understanding of the person of Jesus. In other words, the mystery is revelatory. The mysteries of the Rosary reveal Christ to us and lead us into a fuller understanding of him.

When we look at these mysteries in their Gospel setting, we find that they are Christ-centered. It is a striking fact that the Rosary, the Marian prayer *par excellence*, is taken up almost wholly with the Son of Mary. As the prayer is arranged she is, in a sense, a frame to him – she who once enclosed him in her womb. She does figure in the first two Joyful Mysteries, Annunciation and Visitation, while the last two Glorious Mysteries, Assumption and Queenship, are hers. But in between is all his. The emphasis is as it ought to be.

Because this prayer is biblical it has its priorities right. We find that the Child born of Mary is none other that the Lord, the Savior. Born one of us, he is like us in all things: he suffered and died. The great difference is that 'with his stripes we were healed'; his death won salvation for us. His death was his triumph. The Risen Lord, returned to his Father, his task accomplished, has sent forth the life-giving Spirit. There we have the reality and the purpose of the Incarnation: God became man to make us children of God. 'God sent forth his Son, born of woman ... that we might receive adoption as sons' (Gal. 4:4f). The time had fully come. The Rosary is a prayer of the fulness of time.

The emphasis throughout this book, though not the only concern, is on the theological intent of the biblical writers. This emphasis is not misplaced. Authentic prayer, because it is communion with the true God, must be based on sound theology, on a proper understanding of

God. One is not saying that only a theologian can pray. In fact, theology may inhibit prayer. The Pharisee of Jesus' parable, well versed in the Law, was a theologian of sorts. But his idea of God was false. For him God was a banker who kept a tight account but who owed salvation to one who lived by the Law and thereby stood in the black. One did not really pray to such a God. The poor tax-collector would not have known what theology is, but he did know that God was the God who, in sheer grace, forgave the sinner. His prayer has become our prayer: 'God, be merciful to me, a sinner'. The Rosary is genuine prayer because its basis is theologically firm.

THE JOYFUL MYSTERIES

THE JOYFUL MYSTERIES.

'This day is born to you a Savior who is Christ the Lord'.

The biblical basis of the Rosary is nowhere more evident than in the Joyful Mysteries. Here is no question of a broad gospel background: this first part of the prayer is an echo of one passage — the Infancy Gospel of Luke. The purpose of Luke in this prologue to his gospel is emphatically theological. An appreciation of his purpose reminds us that the Rosary is a Christ-centered prayer. In these first chapters the evangelist is concerned with the birth of the Baptist and with the birth and infancy of Jesus. The Baptist does not enter into the plan of the Rosary; we may look to the other Child alone. And it is abundantly clear that not Mary but her Son holds the stage: she is in the picture because she is *his* mother. This is a mariological truth very much alive in Eastern Christendom: the ikons of Greece and Russia invariably represent the Mother with her Son — she is the Theotokos.

The Lucan message of the Annunciation is the promise of a Child who is Son of God. Elizabeth blesses Mary because of the 'fruit of her womb'. The birth of the Child is described at length. He is presented in the Temple. And the Boy Jesus is found in his Father's house. In all of this, Luke's aim is to present Jesus as transcendent, as a divine Messiah. From his standpoint of faith in the risen

Lord he has looked back and he asserts that the Lord of his christian believing and worship was indeed Lord from the beginning — though men did not perceive it. We witness a development in christological thought.

We find in Mark, and in Matthew and Luke outside of their infancy gospels, a two-stage Christology. This involves the casting of the understanding of the risen Christ, and the titles which express this deepened awareness, back into the gospel accounts of his ministry and passion. In other words, the synoptic gospels reflect the evangelists' perception that the Lord Jesus Christ of their faith-confession, was Lord, too, throughout his ministry. Both Paul and John, each in his own way, pushed the titles and the understanding back to a third stage, thus producing a threefold christological pattern of pre-existence, incarnation, and exaltation. But Matthew and Luke, who do not refer to Jesus' pre-existence, have a three-stage Christology of their own. This is found in their infancy gospels where the understanding of Jesus as Messiah, Savior, and Lord is pushed back to the infancy period. It represents a stage in the developing understanding of him who is the Christian Lord: he is Lord not only in and through the resurrection, not only during his ministry, but also from the very beginning of his earthly existence.

Luke's Infancy Gospel — and the same is true of Matthew's — far from being a grouping of pretty stories, is an important essay in Christology: the understanding of who this Man is. Unlike the other synoptists, Luke regularly calls Jesus, in the period of the ministry, *ho Kyrios* ('the Lord') — it is a conscious use of a christian title. His infancy gospel justifies the use of the title. We see, indeed, that a whole list of titles given to Jesus in these two chapters (Great, Holy, King, Light, Glory, Son of God, Savior, Christ the Lord, Lord) point unmistakably to his unique relationship to the Father. For the most part they are titles that the Old Testament has addressed to Yahweh. In short, we might say that the assimilation of Jesus to Yahweh is the final word of the christology of Luke's infancy gospel.

It must be that the transcendent dignity of Jesus sheds a reflected glow on Mary. Not only that: her role in God's plan is made clear. As Mother of the Messiah she is the true Daughter of Zion where God has come to dwell among his people.

"The Holy Spirit will come upon you,
 and the power of the Most High will overshadow you.
This is why the child to be born will be holy;
 He will be called Son of God" (Lk. 1:35).

THE ANNUNCIATION TO MARY.

'I am the handmaid of the Lord'.

Throughout these two chapters Luke looks to Old Testament language and imagery to convey the atmosphere of this moment before the emergence of Christianity. It is a brilliant achievement on the part of one who himself enjoyed the fullness of christian revelation; but the third evangelist is capable of such artistry. He can turn to divine calls and to angelic messages. The birth of a child of promise is announced to Abraham and Sarah (Gen. 18:9-15), to Hagar (Gen. 16:7-15), to the mother of Samson (Jg. 13:3-20). Moses (Ex. 3:7-12), the prophets (Amos 7:14-15, Isaiah ch. 6, Jeremiah 1:4-10) and, interestingly, Gideon (Jg. 6:11-21) were called by God for a special task and given the assurance of his abiding help. The annunciation to Mary combines these themes: the appearance of this Child of promise will involve the role of Mary as mother of the Messiah.

Vocation.

Luke asserts the basic fact that Mary was called, and knew herself to be called, to be mother of the Messiah. It was, for her, a profound spiritual experience, a matter between herself and her God, something that took place in the depth of her being. In giving external expression to this personal, spiritual experience, Luke spontaneously turned to the Scriptures he knew so well and his writing

has inspired artists down the centuries. He brings before
us the angelic messenger and his message: Gabriel, one of
the 'Angels of the Face' of Jewish tradition, who stand in
the presence of God, and he provides the dialogue to
bring out the significance of the call.

The scene is set in Nazareth, a little Galilean village, an
insignificant place ('Can anything good come out of Nazareth? ' Jn. 1:46), to a young girl of marriageable age.
Indeed, Mary is already betrothed. In Jewish law betroth-
al was a valid and binding contract. But not until the
bridegroom had taken the bride to his home (Mt. 1:24) –
by custom a year after the espousals – did the couple live
as man and wife. In the case of Mary and Joseph this
final step was not taken until some time after the birth of
John the Baptist: from Judea Mary returned to *her* home
(Lk. 1:36). Joseph belonged to the house of David, and
so the legal Davidic descent of Jesus is assured. Though
the term *parthenos* ('virgin') need mean no more than
that Mary was *still* a virgin, Luke's care to tell the reader
twice that Mary was a virgin (1:27) is relevant, as we shall
see, to the manner of Jesus' conception.

The Favored One.

The occurrence, in such a Semitically colored narrative,
of the Greek greeting formula *chaire* ('Hail') instead of
the Semitic 'Peace' (*shalom*) is so surprising that one hesi-
tates to accept it at its face value. On closer inspection
we find that Luke has a specific Old Testament passage in
mind: Zephaniah 3:14-17 – 'Rejoice! Daughter of Zion;
sing aloud, Daughter of Jerusalem! ' (cf Joel 2:21-27;
Zech. 9:9f); The word rendered 'Rejoice' is *chaire* in the
Greek text of Zephaniah, the same term used by the
evangelist. Since that messianic passage of Zephaniah un-
derlies Lk. 1:30f (immediately following) *chaire* in 1:28
must have the meaning 'Rejoice! ' – an invitation to rejoice at the advent of messianic times (for Gabriel's message does herald the new age). In this context, the proper
rendering of *kecharitōmenē* is not the familiar 'full of

grace' but rather the portentous 'Favored One'. The opening words of Gabriel are not a conventional greeting – it is not quite accurate to speak of the 'angelic salutation'. What is announced is that Mary has been chosen to play an essential role in God's plan; she is the object of God's favor because of what is asked of her. And now, too, the statement 'the Lord is with you' falls into place. Coming after 'full of grace' – as this is commonly understood, pointing to Mary's holiness – it is unnecessary, even banal. But once it is recognized that the new name is functional, designating a divinely appointed role, then the assurance that the Lord will be with the chosen one is a guarantee of the effective accomplishment of the divine purpose. Gabriel's opening words, as Luke had understood them, are best rendered: 'Rejoice, O highly Favored One, the Lord is with you'.

You will bear a Son.

Mary herself is 'troubled', perplexed, because she does not yet understand for what purpose and to what extent she has been favored by God. The angel proceeds to enlighten her. His opening words are a close parallel of his initial proclamation:

Rejoice	Fear not
O Favored One	Mary
the Lord is with you.	you have found favor with God.

Next follows the message: the Favored One is to conceive and bear a son and she will give to this son the name of Jesus. The text of Zephaniah is again enlightening:

> The king of Israel, the Lord, is in your midst (literally, in your womb). . .
>
> Fear not Zion. . .
>
> the Lord your God is in your midst (in your womb) (3:15-17).

We notice the same reassuring 'fear not', and the parallel also explains the tautology of Luke: You shall conceive *in your womb* (contrast 1:13) – an echo of a phrase (*beqir-*

bek) which occurs twice in the passage of Zephaniah. Like Hagar (Gen. 16:11) and the mother of Immanuel (Is. 7:14), Mary will name her child: "Jesus" meaning "Yahweh saves".

The angel describes her son and his destiny (1:32f) in terms borrowed from the Old Testament, especially from the oracle of Nathan (2 Sam. 7:12-16), the first in a chain of prophecies in which the Messiah appears as a son of David. In view of this background, the title 'Son of the Most High' and the reference to an everlasting kingdom, do not look beyond the horizon of Jewish messicanic expectation (cf Is. 9:6; Dan. 7:14); It is clear that the son of Mary will be the Messiah but it does not follow that he will be a divine Messiah. At this stage everything is still within the limits of the Old Law, but Luke will go on to explain that the intervention of the Holy Spirit will mean that Jesus must be named 'Son of God' in a new sense.

Virginal Conception.

Like Zechariah (1:18) Mary asks a question — and her question has embarrassed countless commentators. Literally translated from the Greek her question runs: 'How will this be, since I do not know a man?' (1:34) — that is: 'since I have no relations with a man, a husband'. The embarrassment is largely because it had not been recognized that this whole narrative is, ultimately, Luke's composition and the question is his way of moving on to a new and higher level: it marks the change from the Old Testament level of vv. 32f and opens the way for the explanation (v. 35) that what is about to happen is something quite new. In other words, v. 34 is an editorial link-verse. Here Luke is primarily interested in Christology — he is concerned with *what* this Child is going to be.

Luke's assertion of the virginal conception of Jesus is perhaps not quite so evident as we have assumed it to be. It has seemed clear to us because we have read it in the light of the independent infancy gospel of Matthew. However, attention to Luke's carefully balanced presentation of the annunciation to Zechariah of the birth of John the Baptist and the annunciation to Mary of the birth of Jesus, does point in favor of Luke's intention to describe a virginal conception. A patent concern of the parallel accounts is to underline the superiority of Jesus over John the Baptist. The manner of the conception of the Baptist is extraordinary: the power of God overcomes the obstacles of barrenness and old age. If the pattern of superiority is to be maintained, the conception of Jesus must be a greater wonder.

A comparison of the two passages is revealing. In introducing the parents of the Baptist, Luke informs us: 'They had no child, because Elizabeth was barren, and both were advanced in years' (1:7). He has Zechariah repeat this information in Zechariah's question to the angel: 'How shall I know this? For I am an old man and my wife is advanced in years' (1:18). Thus the stage is set for the miraculous conception of John the Baptist. Similarly, in introducing Mary and Joseph, Luke tells us twice that Mary was a virgin (1:27). Mary's question to the angel repeats the information: 'How can this be, since I do not know a man?' (1:34). The stage is set for the more remarkable conception of Jesus. The conception of Jesus must involve the fact that Mary is a virgin just as the conception of the Baptist involved the barrenness of Elizabeth and the advanced age of both parents.

The Holy Spirit.

In our study, centered in Luke's infancy gospel, we do not need to be hidebound and may, readily, turn to Matthew and to his explicit profession of the virginal conception of Jesus. In his "annunciation to Joseph" passage (Mt. 1:18-24) he makes two points: 1) that Jesus was virginally conceived by the action of the Holy Spirit; 2) that Joseph, divinely enlightened, agreed to be his legal father by sanctioning his marriage with Mary and naming the Child. In this manner Jesus is truly 'Son of David' – *despite* his virginal conception. Thus, explicitly in Matthew and, it would appear, explicitly in Luke also, we have a profession of the virginal conception of Jesus. There is no echo of this belief elsewhere in the New Testament but it quickly became a firm datum of christian belief. However, one must endorse the need, in our day, of honestly seeking to grasp what the credal assertion *natus ex Maria virgine* really means. An exegete may fairly maintain that the onus of proof is on those who would argue that the statement does not necessarily demand physical virginity in the conception of Jesus. What is not in doubt is that both Matthew and Luke are primarily interested in the virginal conception as the expression of a christological insight that Jesus was God's son in a unique sense, and from birth. They are interested in the theological import of the assertion.

Son of God.

Again the angel speaks, this time in answer to Mary's question (1:35):

The Holy Spirit will come upon you,
and the power of the Most High will overshadow you.

'Holy Spirit' and 'power of the Most High' stand in parallelism; the Spirit is the divine power or energy. In Is. 11:2 we read that the Spirit of Yahweh will rest on the messianic prince; here the Spirit will come upon her who is to be mother of the Messiah. Already in Gen. 1:2 the Spirit of God hovered over the waters about to perform the great work of creation; here that divine power overshadows Mary, about to perform a new and wonderful creation. In Lk. 1:35b the word *hagion*, 'holy', causes some difficulty. The verse might be rendered:

That is why the child to be born will be holy;
he will be called Son of God.

The presence of 'holy', which occurs, also unexpectedly, in 2:23, is due to the influence of Dan. 9 in the one case and of Mal. 3 in the other. In Dan. 9:24 the messianic age will be marked, among other ways, by the consecration of a Holy One. With this 'Holy One' in mind, in v. 35 Luke insinuates that the angel's message was the signal for the inauguration of the messianic age. In v. 32 we have noted that 'Son of the Most High' is a title within the Jewish messianic perspective and does not necessarily imply transcendence. Here the situation is quite other: *dio kai*, 'that is why', points back to the exclusive action of God. The Holy One will be Son of God in a new manner, in a unique sense.

Fiat.

In accordance with the literary form of angelic message, Mary, like Gideon (Jg. 6:17,21) and like Zechariah (Lk. 1:18-20), is given a sign, a guarantee of the authenticity of the message – though, in her case, the sign is unsolicited. Luke's v. 37 is an almost verbatim quotation of God's words to Abraham in relation to the promised birth of Isaac (Gen. 18:14). In Mary's consent,

> Behold, I am the handmaid of the Lord;
> let it be to me according to your word

we may see the true pattern of her humility. If she had been troubled, and if she had asked a question (and we can trust the delicate perception of Luke) it is because she had been perplexed. Now that she knows the divine purpose she accepts that purpose unhesitatingly and with perfect simplicity. If heroics would be out of place at such a moment so, no less certainly, would be a protestation, even a suggestion of unworthiness. Mary was too completely God's to think of herself at all. Here, supremely, Luke displays the sensitivity and psychological perception he shows throughout his gospel.

Faith.

Mary was now aware of the divine purpose – but did she understand it? Above all, did she realize that the child to be born of her would be divine? We know that the intimate disciples had not grasped this truth during the lifetime of their Master; it needed the resurrection to open their eyes. We have good reason to ask if Mary was aware, from the beginning, of the divinity of her Son. If we look at the essentials of Luke's narrative, we see that his attention first bears on the child whose birth he announces, then on the motherhood of Mary, and lastly on the manner of her maternity. In other words, the central fact, and the source of the others, is the Incarnation; and this, by definition, means that God became Man. This is the reality, but it is independent of any human perception of it. The gospels make it clear that the disciples came to understand who their Master was only on the other side of the resurrection. There is no reason to suppose that it was any different with Mary. We shall see that Elizabeth draws attention to her *faith*. She is one who lived by faith, who lived in the darkness that is a necessary feature of faith. And surely if Jesus, 'like his brethren in every respect' (Heb. 2:17), the 'High Priest who fulfills our need' lived a fully human life, nothing less can be asked of his mother. 'Blessed is she who believed'. – she is the Woman of faith, and thereby she is, eminently, our Mother.

"*My being proclaims the greatness of the Lord
my spirit finds in God my savior,
For he has looked upon his servant; in her loneliness;
all ages to come shall call me blessed*" (Lk. 1:46-48).

THE VISITATION.

'Blessed is she who believed'.

This narrative serves as a hinge between the two Birth stories, of John and of Jesus. And this meeting of women illustrates their respective situations. Elizabeth's pregnancy was not only a sign for Mary; it was also an invitation. She set off, at once, for a 'city of Judah'. In view of the determination 'hill country' it must be in the neighborhood of Jerusalem; a tradition going back to the sixth century points to the delightfully situated village of *Ain Karim*, five miles west of the city. The 'haste' of Mary was inspired by friendship and charity. The journey would have taken some four days.

Blessed is she who believed.

At Mary's greeting Elizabeth felt the infant move in her womb (cf Gen. 25:22) as an inspired prophetess ('filled with the Holy Spirit') she understood that he had leaped for joy at the presence of the mother of the Messiah. What did happen is that the Baptist's mother was also able to perceive a special significance in an occurrence, the movement of an infant in the womb, that she would otherwise have regarded as fortuitous. But Luke gives us to understand that the child is filled with messianic joy – he uses the verb *skirtaō* ('to leap for joy') as in 6:23. Through this debut of his prophetic career the Precursor fulfills the promise made by the angel to Zechariah: 'he will be filled with the Holy Spirit, even from his mother's womb' (1:15).

Enlightened by the Holy Spirit, Elizabeth is aware of Mary's secret: she is the mother of her Lord. 'Lord' could designate the Messiah; but Luke throughout his gospel regularly gives to Jesus the christian title *ho kyrios* ('the Lord'). He means it to have this fuller sense on the lips of Elizabeth. Mother and infant have recognized and acknowledged the Mother of the Lord, have discerned it in the voice of Mary, the words of her greeting. As Mother of the Lord, Mary is 'blessed among women', a hebraism (cf Jd. 13:18) meaning the most blessed of all women. Elizabeth went on to praise Mary's unhesitating acquiescence in God's plan for her — her great faith: 'blessed is she who believed'.

Magnificat.

Mary's reply is her *Magnificat*. This hymn is the conclusion of, and the interpretation of, Luke's Visitation scene. In form a thanksgiving psalm, the Magnificat is a chain of Old Testament reminiscences and leans especially on the canticle of Hannah (1 Sam. 2:1-10). Because of its heavy borrowing it is not of great poetic quality. Furthermore, there is no clear reference to the messianic birth — and this is surprising in view of the angel's message and the words of Elizabeth. And 'humiliation' (the normal meaning of *tapeinōsis*, 1:48, rather than 'humility', 'lowliness') does not apply very well to the young Virgin. The Magnificat is a psalm that has come to Luke from the circle of the 'poor of Yahweh', the saints of Judaism. The *anawim*, or 'poor', assumed a large place in the religious life of Israel after the Exile. The term reflects an attitude of mind: a willing openness to God, humility before God (cf Zeph. 2:3; 3:11f; Lk. 6:20): the poor man (*anaw*) is regarded as Yahweh's client, one who abandons himself wholly to God and puts his trust in him. It is easy to understand that a psalm from such a milieu would already marvellously conform to the sentiments of this 'handmaid of the Lord' (Lk. 1:38). The psalm was doubtless first put in the mouth of the Daughter of Zion, she who in the prophets, is the spouse of Yahweh, tested, humiliated, helped, and redeemed, giving birth to the messianic people (Is. 54:1; 66:7-12; Mi. 4:10; Jer. 4:31) and to the Messiah (Is. 7:14; Mi. 5:1f). It thus fits Mary in whom Luke sees the anti-typical fulfillment of the Daughter of Zion (cf Lk. 1:28; 2:35). The Magnificat stands between the Old Testament and the New and, like the rest of Luke's infancy gospel, captures the atmosphere of that unique moment. Luke presents the canticle as a song of Mary and we may, and should, read it in this light.

Elizabeth had blessed Mary as mother of the Messiah; Mary gives the glory, in joyful thanksgiving, to the God who had blessed her, and through her, Israel: 'My soul magnifies the Lord'. The rest of the opening cry of joy (Lk. 1:47) echoes the words of Habakkuk: 'I will rejoice in the Lord, I will joy in the God of my salvation' (Hab. 3:18). God has looked with favor upon his handmaid, upon her who is the most perfect of the 'poor of Yahweh'. Her total acceptance of God's will has won for her, the Favored One, everlasting glory. At once, she turns the attention away from herself, to the Almighty, the holy and merciful God, who has done great things for her. The Mighty One shows his power most of all in caring for the needy. In truth, 'the steadfast love of the Lord is from everlasting to everlasting upon those who fear him' (Ps. 103:17). All mankind will find hope in what God has achieved in Mary: loneliness turned into fruitfulness.

The humble exalted.

The interest then (vv. 51-53) switches to Israel and to the manifestation of God's power, holiness and goodness in favor of his people. These verses are not concerned with the past, or not with the past only, but represent God's action at all times: what he has done to Mary and what he, through her as mother of the Messiah, has done for Israel, shows forth his manner of acting. He does mighty deeds with his arm, the symbol of his power, when he reverses human situations — the proud, the mighty, and the rich he has humbled and left empty, while he has lifted up and blessed with good things the poor of this world (the *anawim*). None of this, of course, is brought about by a social revolution which sets one in place of the other; the change follows on God's attitude toward those who ask humbly and those who believe that they have the right to demand. The great reversal is finally effected in the perfect stage of the kingdom, the life to come.

The closing verses (1:54-55) in the mouth of Mary, point to the final intervention of God. His sending of the Messiah is the final act of his gracious treatment of Israel, the people which, through his covenant with Abraham (Gen. 17:7), had become his 'Servant' (Is. 41:8f). Mindful of his great mercy, he has fulfilled the promise made to the patriarch: a promise made to one man is accomplished in a woman, the Daughter of Zion.

The concluding verse (1:56) has often been misunderstood. Though Luke immediately begins to describe the birth of John (v. 57), it does not follow, as it seems it must, that Mary had departed before Elizabeth's child was born. Typically (cf 1:64-67; 3:19f; 8:37f), the evangelist is rounding off one theme before passing to another. The Visitation did close with the departure of Mary, so he mentions it at the end; the birth of John is a distinct episode. We may surely take for granted that our Lady remained as long as Elizabeth had need of her: she *the* handmaid of the Lord, was happy to serve others. Mary returned 'to her home', that is to say, she had not yet begun to live with Joseph.

"She gave birth to her first-born son
and wrapped him in swaddling clothes
and laid him in a manger, because there was no room
for them in the place where travelers lodged" (Lk.
2:7).

THE BIRTH OF JESUS.

'I bring you good news of a great joy'.

While Matthew simply mentions the birth of Jesus Christ (Mt. 2:1), Luke gives a detailed description of it. Throughout the first chapter of his gospel, while dealing with the annunciation to Zechariah and Mary and with the birth of the Baptist, Luke's narrative has remained within the ambit of the Jewish world. Now, at the beginning of the second chapter, when he comes to the birth of him who is a 'light for revelation to the Gentiles' (2:32) his perspective opens, if only for a moment, on to the Gentile world. His eyes have glanced from the Jerusalem of the beginning of his gospel to the Rome of the last chapter of Acts. The birth of the Savior of all men is fixed – though perhaps too vaguely for our taste – on the calendar of world history.

An imperial decree.

It may be that the serious difficulty raised by Luke's reference to a census of Quirinius is due to our taking him too literally. Luke makes the census emanate from the Emperor himself and depicts Joseph submitting to the imperial edict – even with the hardship of Mary being in the final stage of pregnancy. In this way, he already makes the point, sustained throughout Acts, that Christianity from the very beginning was never a threat to Rome. He also shows how the great Augustus, unwittingly, plays a role in God's plan. Through his decree it came to pass that Jesus the Messiah was born in the town of David.

When we look at it dispassionately, we must admit that what we had taken to be the Lucan picture of the many distant descendants of David crowding into the insignificant Bethlehem, is not very likely — still less likely as following on a policy of the practical Romans. The difficulty may well be due to our reading of Luke's text. Here again one may look to the independent witness of Matthew, for he gives the impression that Bethlehem was the habitual home of Joseph. In his narrative Nazareth appears only as a place of refuge from Archelaus (2:22f), otherwise Joseph would normally have returned to Judea. If Joseph were a native of Bethlehem the census picture is more reasonable. While the gathering there of all the descendants of David is hard to imagine, the presence of a resident like Joseph is normal. Lack of room in the *katalygma* raises no difficulty: it is not an 'inn' (in Lk. 10:34 the word is *pandocheion*) but the common room of Joseph's family home. The room was so crowded that no better place than a manger could be found as a resting place for the babe.

The "first-born".

Joseph, though a native of Bethlehem, at this time resided at Nazareth; he went, with Mary, to his former home. There is some difficulty about Luke's referring to Mary as Joseph's 'betrothed'; perhaps Luke is delicately hinting that Joseph was not the father of Jesus. The expression 'first-born son' has in mind (or echoes) the law prescribing the dedication of the first-born male to God (Ex. 13:12; 34:19; cf Lk. 2:23); an only son is 'first-born' in this technical sense.

Since we are told that the new-born baby was laid in a manger, we learn that Joseph and Mary, perhaps in search of privacy more than anything else, found shelter in a stable of some sort. A tradition going back to the second-century Justin Martyr, specifies a cave. These circumstances emphasize the lowliness and poverty that surrounded the birth of Jesus: nothing here suggests the power and glory of his divinity. The observation that Mary, by herself, wrapped the infant in swaddling clothes, is to be understood in the same sense. Yet, Luke's delicate touch is far removed from the heavy-handed treatment of the apocryphal gospels, whose authors lose no opportunity of emphasizing the virginity of Mary and the wonder of the birth. Throughout the infancy narrative it does seem that Luke is convinced of the virginity of Mary, but nowhere does this fact obtrude.

The Poor.

In Lk. 7:22 we learn that one of the signs given to the Baptist whereby he might know that Jesus was indeed the Messiah was that 'the poor have the good news preached to them'. It is the climactic sign and so it is fitting that the first announcement of Jesus' birth was made to simple shepherds: these, the poor and humble, despised by the orthodox as non-observers of the Law, are granted and accept the revelation which the leaders of Israel will reject. Bethlehem lies at the edge of the desert of Judea and the shepherds, living in the open, were nomads — like the bedouin of today who frequent the same desert region. An angel suddenly appeared to a group of them as they guarded their flocks by night, and they found themselves surrounded by a brilliant light: the 'glory of the Lord', an expression frequent in the Old Testament (cf Ex. 13:21; 16:10), accompanies a heavenly manifestation. 'Fear', religious awe, was their natural reaction.

The Savior.

Just like Zechariah and Mary, the shepherds, too, were reassured. The angel's message is a proclamation of good news (*euaggelizomai*, 'to proclaim good news', is a favorite word of Luke) and joy to all the people of Israel; for, despite the initial setting of the birth of Jesus in the framework of world history (2:1), the universalist note is

not again struck in this episode (as it will be in 2:32) and
the horizon closes on the limits of the Jewish world. 'This
day' — the long-awaited day of Israel's salvation — has
dawned; a new-born child is the Savior (*sōtēr* is used of
Jesus only here in the synoptics, but Luke employs it
again in Acts 5:31; 13:23) who has brought salvation.
This Savior is 'Christ the Lord' — the title *Christos Kyrios*
is found only once in the Septuagint, the ancient Greek
translation of the Old Testament (Lamentations 4:20) and
nowhere else in the New Testament. He is the Messiah en-
dowed with authority and having dominion. Again like
Zechariah (1:18,20) and Mary (1:26), the shepherds are
given a sign: 'Let them go and see for themselves that
they are not the victims of illusion; they shall find a child
in a manger, not left naked and abandoned as they might
expect to find a child who had been put in such an odd
cradle, but properly clothed in swaddling bands' (La-
grange).

Peace on earth.

The presence of the 'glory of the Lord' (v. 9) had already assured the shepherds that something wonderful
was afoot; now they hear the singing of a heavenly choir
— thus has Luke brought out the true dimension of a
moment of simplicity.

> Glory to God in the highest heavens
> and peace on earth to men who enjoy his favor.

It appears that this canticle of the angels, like the Benedictus and Magnificat, had come to Luke from the same
Jewish milieu as they. It would seem that 'Glory to God'
expresses not so much a wish ('let God be glorified') as a
statement, a recognition of the significance of the hour,
an acknowledgment of the saving act of God. The familiar
translation of *eudokias*, peace to men 'of good will', referring to human goodness, fails to convey the true meaning;
the renderings 'with whom he is pleased' and 'who enjoy
his favor', pointing to the divine benevolence, suit the
term and the context. In biblical thought, God alone is

the source of man's goodness. This is the thrust of the words of Jesus to the man who had addressed him as 'Good Teacher': 'Why do you call me good? No one is good but God alone' (Mk. 10:18). The sense of the angel's canticle is that, in the birth of the Messiah, God is glorified, his power and his mercy are manifest, and, on earth, the men whom he loves (people like Simeon and Anna) receive the divine blessing of peace, the peace which the savior has brought.

Marvelling at their strange experience, stirred to excited anticipation by the angels' word, the shepherds set out in haste to Bethlehem. There they discovered that the facts were just as the angel had described. Naturally, they spoke freely of what they had seen, and of the things that had been told them. Inevitably, if anything of this had come to the ears of 'the wise' they put no stock in the 'illusions' of these simple men. But one, at least, forgot none of these happenings: Mary kept in her heart the events and words and pondered over them (cf 2:51). Luke is, perhaps, reminding us that she is the ultimate source of his Infancy Gospel. More to the point, his words imply that her understanding of these events was not complete; she had to ponder them in the quiet of her heart. In his customary manner, Luke winds up the episode by indicating the return of the shepherds to their flocks. They went on their way, 'glorifying and praising God': joyful thanksgiving is a favorite theme of his.

The splendor of angelic manifestation and heavenly glory at his birth was not reflected in the person of Jesus: he is the infant, lying helpless in a manger, a babe who must be circumcised on the eight day (2:21); It was a father's right to name his child and in this case, too, the heavenly Father had bestowed the name, indicated beforehand by the angel (1:31). The name Jesus ('Yahweh saves') suits perfectly the character of this Savior revealed to the shepherds, he who is Christ the Lord.

Matthew wrote his infancy gospel independently of the Lucan infancy gospel. The two narratives are not quite at

one but, in view of this, their agreement in the essential
data is all the more impressive. The most important factor
is that Matthew's purpose, too, in this prologue to his
gospel, is firmly theological. And it is here that the christological insights of the evangelists meet.

Son of David.

Even in the infancy gospel, as throughout Matthew's
work, there is an interest in community: from the beginning Jesus Messiah is the representative of God's people
and, in his life, reflects the history of Israel. The evangelist has set out to answer the double questions: *Who* is
Jesus and *how* has he come into the world? (ch. 1).
Whence did he come and *where* was he born? (ch. 2).
Matthew's genealogy (1:1-17) does not seek to prove the
Davidic descent of Jesus; it has, rather, the theological
intent of situating him within the divine plan of salvation:
he emerges as the heir and as the fulfillment of God's
purpose. The passage 1:18-24 (the annunciation to Joseph) answers the question raised by v. 16 of the genealogy ('Joseph, the husband of Mary, of whom Jesus was
born, who is called Christ'). It makes two points: that
Jesus was virginally conceived by the action of the Holy
Spirit, and that Joseph, divinely enlightened, became the
legal father of the child. In this way Jesus is truly 'son of
David'. Having thus presented the Messiah, Jesus, in the
light of his virginal and Davidic birth, Matthew goes on
the depict his mission in an aura of light and of suffering.
In anecdotic form he conveys what Luke has done
through the mouth of Simeon (Lk. 2:34f – 'this child is
set for the fall and rising of many'): the call of the
pegans to salvation (the Magi), crisis and rejection in
Israel (massacre of the innocents, flight into Egypt, obscu-
rity in Nazareth). All of these episodes are centered in
biblical texts which bring out their theological significance.

Son of God.

In the Magi from the East, guided by the Star (Num.

24:17 — 'A star shall arise out of Jacob') and adoring Jesus in Bethlehem (Micah. 2:6), Matthew sees the pagan world attracted by the light of the Messiah and coming to pay homage to the 'king of the Jews' in the city of David. The homage is described with the help of the scriptural theme of the kings of Arabia bringing their presents to the King Messiah (Is. 60:1-6; Ps. 72:10f,15). In the Flight into Egypt, Matthew's interest bears on the return involved: he quotes Hos. 11:1 — 'Out of Egypt have I called my son'. He sees in the episode a parallel to the Exodus which makes the infancy of Jesus a symbolic accomplishment of the destiny of Israel. Jesus is the Son *par excellence* truly meriting the title 'son' already given to Israel. In calling him from the land of exile, God calls together with him the messianic people of which he is the inclusive representative (Mt. 1:1-17). His return is the divine guarantee of the deliverance many times promised.

The Nazarene.

The citation of Jer. 31:15 enables Matthew to evoke, beyond the massacre of Bethlehem infants (Mt. 2:13-18), the Babylonian Exile; this great crisis in the history of Israel has its reflection in the destiny of the child Jesus. The comparison of Jesus with Moses, frequent in the New Testament, is evident in Mt. 2:19-23 for v. 20 echoes Ex. 4:19 — like Moses, Jesus can return after the death of those who have sought his life. Here again Matthew's chief interest is in the prophetic oracle (2:23); In *Nazōraios* ('He shall be called a Nazarene') he probably sees an echo of the Hebrew participle *nasur* ('preserved') as an allusion to the Servant of the Lord (Is. 42:6) and to the messianic Remnant (Is. 49:6 — 'the preserved of Israel'). Jesus, for Matthew, is thus the antitype of the Remnant come back from the Exile in humble circumstances, but yet preserved by God as the hope of messianic salvation.

In his infancy gospel Matthew has shown that the son born to Mary is indeed the Son of David but he has shown, too, that beyond this, he is the Son of God. For the Son of Mary conceived by the Holy Spirit (1:18-20) is to save his people from their sins (1:21) and is named by God himself (in Scripture) 'God-with-us' (1:22f). At 2:15 God declares: 'Out of Egypt have I called *my Son*'. It is the same Son of whom he had said: he will shepherd 'my people' Israel. A christological truth stands forth: Jesus, the Messiah, is the Son of God, the eschatological Shepherd who will save God's people from their sins.

"Now Master, you can dismiss your servant in peace;
   you have fulfilled your word.
For my eyes have witnessed your saving deed
   displayed for all the people to see" (Lk. 2:29-31).

THE PRESENTATION OF JESUS
IN THE TEMPLE.

'My eyes have seen your salvation'.

In 2:22-24 Luke has combined two requirements of the Law: the purification of the mother after childbirth and the redemption of the first-born, who must be consecrated to the Lord. Thus, somewhat loosely, he can speak of 'their' purificaiton — that is, of Mary and Jesus. It is convenient to consider the prescriptions separately for they are, in fact, distinct.

According to Lev. 12:2-4, a mother was purified forty days after the birth of a son; she was required to make an offering of a lamb for a burnt offering and a young pigeon or turtledove for a sin offering. A poor woman could substitute another pigeon for the lamb (Lev. 12:6-8); Mary's offering was the offering of the poor. The 'purification' regarded strictly ritual uncleanness and did not, of course, imply a moral fault of childbirth. Mary, like her Son, fulfilled the observances of the Law, even to the making of a sin offering. Jesus is 'born of a woman, born under the law' (Gal. 4:4) — but precisely 'to redeem those who were under the law, so that we might receive adoption as sons' (4:5).

If Luke has mentioned the purification of Mary it is only because it happened to be associated with the presentation of Jesus in the Temple. The first-born son (he

'that opens the womb') belonged to the Lord (Ex.
13:2,12) but was redeemed, bought back, by the payment
of a stipulated sum (Num. 18:15f). Luke, significantly,
says nothing about Jesus being bought back – for he already belonged to his Father. It is nowhere laid down in
the Law that the first-born must be taken to the Temple
and presented there. In this case, the episode is entirely
credible seeing that Bethlehem is a mere five miles from
Jerusalem. And the fact that Jesus was so presented is
obviously of great importance for Luke. Here again, the
Old Testament background helps him to convey the true
meaning of this simple scene.

Holy to the Lord.

In v. 23 – 'Every male that opens the womb shall be
called holy to the Lord' – *hagion*, 'holy', is unexpected.
The verse is a rather free combination of Ex. 13:2,12 but
the word 'holy', which does not occur in the Exodus
text, has come from Luke, who had inserted it also at
1:35b – 'therefore the child to be born will be called
holy'. Its presence in the latter case is due to the influence of Dan. 9:24 – the consecration of a 'Holy One'
which will mark the inauguration of the messianic age –
while its occurrence in 2:23 establishes a contact between
Dan. 9 and another messianic text, Mal. 3, for this last
text stands behind Luke's description of the Presentation.
Since in 1:16f and in the Benedictus he presents the
Baptist as the messenger, the Elijah, who will prepare the
way of Yahweh (Mal. 3:1,23), it must follow that the
'Holy One' who is presented in the Temple is none other
than the *Lord*: 'Behold, I send my messenger to prepare
the way before me, and the Lord whom you seek will
suddenly come to his Temple' (Mal. 3:1). In such a subtle
and sophisticated manner does the evangelist propose his
christology.

The Prophet.

It was fitting that the Lord, on entering his Temple for
the first time, should be greeted by a representative of

the prophets. This role was filled by Simeon, the righteous and devout, who awaited, with faith and patience, the fulfillment of the hope of Israel, its 'consolation' (cf Is. 40:1; 49:13; 51:12; 61:2). The Holy Spirit had assured him that he would not die until he had seen the Messiah. Now the Spirit had moved him to visit the Temple and had revealed to him that the infant who was at this moment being presented there was indeed the longed-for Messiah.

The prophecy of Simeon (1:29-35) is rhytmic, at least in its first part (1:29-32), but it fits the situation too well to be derived from an older hymn. This first part is the *Nunc Dimittis*, a canticle which like the Magnificat and Benedictus, is used daily in the liturgy. Simeon realizes that, in view of the fulfillment of the promise made to him (v. 26), death must be near; he can die in peace, like Abraham (Gen. 15:15), but more privileged than Abraham. His cup of joy is filled to overflowing because he has gazed upon the 'salvation of God', the Messiah whom God has sent to save his people. And not his own people only: the Gentiles are destined for salvation too (2:29-32; cf Is. 52:10; 42:6; 49:6). This messianic salvation is not only a beacon which shines before the nations, it is a brightness which dissipates the darkness and enlightens them. But since salvation comes from Israel (cf Jn. 4:22), and was made manifest through the chosen people, it redounds to the glory of Israel. In this passage, for the first time in the infancy gospel, we look explicitly (cf Lk. 2:1) beyond Jewish limits to a universalist horizon — salvation for all men; but still the perspective is that of the Old Testament, the vision of Second Isaiah. The call of the pagans to the light of salvation through the intermediary of Israel is the program of the prophets which Jesus has striven to realize, despite the resistance of the Jews.

The Sign of Contradiction.

Though this infant has come as the Savior of his people, he will be rejected by many of them (cf Jn. 1:11), for he will stand as a sign of contradiction, a stone that can be stumbling-block (Is. 8:14f) or cornerstone (Is. 28:16) according as men turn their backs on him or accept him (Lk. 2:34f). In his business there can be no neutrality, for he is the light that men cannot ignore (cf Jn. 9:39; 12:44,50), the light that reveals their inmost thoughts and forces them to take part for him or against him. Here, again, Mary is the Daughter of Zion: the sword that will pierce her soul, her inmost being, is the heart—rending of the Daughter of Zion by sword-thrusts of Yahweh devastating the land but sparing a small Remnant (cf Ezek. 14:17, 21-23; 12:14, 16). In Luke's mind, the sword that will divide Israel, consuming the wicked and leaving Mary and the faithful remnant un-harmed, is the revealing word (Heb. 3:12f) brought by Jesus. We may see, too, in the enigmatic words of Simeon, a veiled presage of the great sorrow which was to be Mary's in full measure when she stood at the foot of the Cross (Jn. 19:23-27).

The Prophetess.

After a prophet a prophetess — the delicate hand of Luke — and, yet again (implicitly this time) the Spirit of prophecy. Anna, now eighty-four, having lost her husband seven years after an early marriage, had preferred to remain a widow. She practically lived in the Temple, so uninterrupted were her prayers. A typical saint of Ju-daism, one of the *anawim*, the 'poor of Yahweh', she is also an example to christian widows (cf 1 Tim. 5:5,9). Her prophetic instinct enabled her to recognize the infant Messiah and, gratefully, she spoke of him to those who, like Simeon and herself, looked for the salvation of Jeru-salem (Is. 52:9), that is, of Israel, God's people.

The return to Nazareth of Jesus and his parents (v. 39) serves to round off Luke's narrative. As at the close of the Baptist's infancy narrative (1:80) so here (2:40) we find a 'refrain of growth'. Growth and development was not only physical but intellectual as well: though 'filled with wisdom', Jesus grew in wisdom daily (2:52). His wisdom is exemplified in the next scene.

"On the third day they came upon him in the temple
sitting in the midst of the teachers, listening
to them and asking them questions. All who heard him
were amazed at his intelligence and his answers"
(Lk. 2:46-47).

THE FINDING OF JESUS IN THE TEMPLE.

'Did you not know that I must be in my Father's house?'

The two chapters of Luke's infancy gospel are dominated by the idea of messianic fulfillment. The different scenes build up to the climax of the entry into the Temple, with its pendant: the 'finding' of Jesus in his Father's house. This incident of the boy Jesus lost, and found in the Temple (2:41-50), had taken on the form of a pronouncement story, having its point in the question of Jesus (v. 49). The Law obliged all men who had reached the age of puberty to go to the Temple three times yearly – for the feasts of Passover, Pentecost, and Tabernacles (Ex. 23:14-17; 34:23f; Dt. 16:16f). Women and children were not bound by this law (but women did freely accompany their husbands) and the law itself was not observed in the letter by those at some distance from Jerusalem: an annual journey to one feast sufficed in practice. Rabbinical ruling had it that a boy was not bound to make the pilgrimage before the completion of his thirteenth year, but it was customary for the parents to take him with them at an earlier age. The text does not necessarily imply that this was Jesus' first visit to the Temple (apart from 2:22).

It was not obligatory to remain for the whole term of the feast (here the seven days of Unleavened Bread), but

most pilgrims would have remained until the close of the
Passover festival. As a Jewish boy of twelve, Jesus was
well able to look after himself and his parents would
naturally have taken for granted that he was with one of
the scattered groups of the returning Nazareth caravan.
Usually the pilgrims set off on the return journey late in
the day and the first stage would have been a short one
of, perhaps, some hours – the 'day's journey' (v. 44) need
not be taken literally. When it had become clear to
Joseph and Mary that the boy was not with the caravan
they returned to Jerusalem, searching for him.

In my Father's house.

At last they found him, 'after three days', that is, on
the third day (cf Mk. 8:31), sitting among the scribes, the
teachers of the Law. It was customary for the rabbis to
teach in the surroundings of the Temple; their pupils sat
on the ground 'at the feet' of their teacher, as Paul had
sat before Gamaliel (Acts 22:3). But here we are presented rather with a learned discussion among a group of
rabbis, one which naturally attracted some attention. The
intelligent and searching questions of Jesus won him a
hearing and these 'teachers of Israel' (Jn. 3:10) were soon
lost in wonderment at the unusual wisdom of this twelve-
year-old boy.

The relief of his parents was intense – *exeplegēsen*,
'they were overcome' – and Mary's reproach was the
spontaneous expression of the pain she had suffered.
Jesus' query, the first and only words of his recorded in
these chapters, might be paraphrased: 'Where would you
expect a child to be but in his father's house?'. The
phrase, *en tois tou patros mou* (literally, 'in the things of
my Father') could mean 'about my Father's affairs', but
the far more satisfactory rendering is 'in my Father's
house'; the French *chez mon père* is quite like the Greek
phrase. It follows that the claims of this Father must
override all other demands; his mission will break the
natural ties of family (cf Mk. 3:31-35). Furthermore, the

episode may be regarded as a prolongation of the Presentation: the child who had been presented is now, as Son of God, at home in the Temple. The close of the Infancy gospel anticipates the close of the Gospel: Jesus, now in the house of his Father (v. 49), will, by the way of his glorification — his passion, death, resurrection, and ascension (chs. 23-24) — return to his Father. His last words are an echo of his first words: 'Father, into thy hands I commit my spirit' (23:46): he will abide with his Father forever (cf 9:51). The full implication of the Boy's words was not immediately apparent and unfolded gradually: 'and they did not understand the saying which he spoke to them' (2:50). This points, as clearly as one could wish, to Mary's limited understanding of her Son.

He was obedient to them.

The hour for the breaking of family ties was not yet; until the beginning of his public ministry Jesus was to remain quietly in Nazareth, a dutiful son. 'Though he was in the form of God... he emptied himself, taking the form of a servant' (Phil. 2:6f). Mary's pondering on these *rhēmata*, events and words (v. 19), surely brought a growth in her understanding of the mystery of her Son. It was a gradual process which needed, for its full flowering, the light of the resurrection. If we must insist on the full humanity of Jesus — including human limitations — we should certainly not attempt to make Mary less human, especially in face of the plain statements of Scripture.

The 'refrain of growth', an echo of v. 40, underlines the complementary aspect of the Finding in the Temple, from the literary point of view. This verse (2:52) is practically a quotation of 1 Sam. 2:26. Luke has quite deliberately marked the physical development of Jesus: *to brephos*, 'the baby' (2:16), *to paidion*, 'the child' (v. 40), *Iēsous ho pais*, 'the boy Jesus' (v. 43), *Iēsous* (v. 52). In this final verse we learn that his human understanding too deepened and matured. The reality of the incarnation, the authentic humanity of Jesus, demanded such growth, but also set limits to his human knowledge; again Scripture is formal (cf Heb. 2:17; 4:15; 5:7; Mk. 13:32). As God looked with complaceny on his Incarnate Son who also attracted the favor of men (cf Prov. 3:4). The Infancy Gospel, which has subtly intimated the divine status of the Messiah, closes with an emphatic assertion of the reality of Jesus' humanity.

THE SORROWFUL MYSTERIES

THE SORROWFUL MYSTERIES.

'Was it not necessary that the Christ should suffer these things. . .?'

The different 'mysteries', from Gethsemane to the Cross, are so many links that string together the episodes of the Passion Story. We will look, not to these isolated moments, but to the whole drama. In presenting the passion and death of Jesus each evangelist has his own emphasis. Mark is preoccupied with an understanding of Christ prevalent, or at least present, in his community, which looked only to glory and ignored the Cross. He paints a stark picture and emphasizes that the disciples of a suffering Messiah must be prepared to suffer. Matthew, conscious of the conflict between Judaism and his largely Jewish-Christian community, stresses the role of official Judaism in bringing about the death of Jesus. Luke, here too as throughout his gospel, highlights the compassion and boundless love of Jesus. John's passion-narrative is a sophisticated drama of the royal progress of the incarnate Son of God.

These varied viewpoints give us a richer understanding of the suffering and death of our Savior. While not morbidly lingering over the stark and painful details, we do encounter a Man who shrank from suffering but found, in prayer, the strength to face calmly a horrible death. He was mocked, maltreated, scourged: the butt of malice and of thoughtless cruelty. We are reminded that the disciples of a suffering Messiah cannot expect to be free of suffering; in our little measure we must share his Gethsemane, his contumely, and his Calvary. And we must, sadly, recognize ourselves, in the disciples who fled away and left him alone. We can find hope in the thief who, even on an earned gibbet, heard a promise of blessedness. We can receive strength from the steadfastness of Her who stood by the Cross.

We see, too, that the story of Jesus did not end with the grave. John's narrative is instinct with theological truth. Jesus is indeed a King and his Cross was his throne. To eyes of flesh his death was abject failure. To eyes of faith his death was triumph. The lesson in unmistakable. Here and here alone is christian victory. Yet, we need to learn this lesson. We are so prone to measure the things of God by the standards of the world. Paul had learned the lesson: he would resolutely preach Christ crucified, though the message of the Cross be foolishness and scandal. Our Lord is King, but not as the great ones of this world. He had come, not to be served but to serve and to lay down his life for us. His death is the last word of God's love.

"He withdrew from them about a stone's throw, then went down on his knees and prayed in these words: 'Father, if it is your will, take this cup from me; yet not my will but yours be done'" (Lk. 22:41-42).

THE AGONY IN THE GARDEN.

'And being in an agony he prayed more earnestly'.

'And when they had sung a hymn, they went out to the Mount of Olives' (Mk. 14:26). The Last Supper had taken place: Jesus had given himself to his disciples, and to all of us. Then, having sung the psalms that made up the Hallel which closed the Passover feast, Jesus and his disciples set out for the Mount of Olives. He warned them of failure in the face of their confidence in their own steadfastness (14:27-31). His declaration, 'But after I am raised up, I will go before you to Galilee' (14:28) is meant to prepare for the commission of 16:7 — 'But go, tell his disciples and Peter that he is going before you into Galilee'. Set directly after a prophecy of a scattering of the disciples (14:27), v. 28 must refer to their gathering again. It refers to a new relationship of Shepherd and sheep which follows on the resurrection; the crucified and risen Christ will draw together those who had failed him. For, the new Israel seemed to have melted away at its very inception. 'It had indeed melted away, and there was nothing to show for all the work that had been done, until it was re-created by an act of forgiveness. This was the emergence of the new Israel, of which the prophets had spoken in terms of resurrection from the grave. That was how the Church was brought into existence, and it

could never forget that its foundation members were
discredited men who owed their position solely to the
magnanimity of their ill-used Master' (C. H. Dodd).

Agony.

Jesus and his disciples made their way to Gethsemane.
'He took with him Peter and James and John' (14:33) —
the three privileged disciples. Usually Jesus prayed alone
but it was necessary that the Twelve, at least these three,
should have witnessed the final combat of their Master,
and should have shared in it in some measure, if they
were to accept with him, as his companions, the cross
which he offers. The phrase, 'and he began to be greatly
distressed and troubled' is strong even for Mark. In contrast with the martyrs who faced death with serenity (but
to what extent is their unruffled approach to death really
due to the hagiographer?), Jesus is said to be deeply
troubled and distressed — how human, and how comforting. Heaven save us from man's portrayal of what man
should be in favor of the divine portrayal of what man is.
The candid testimony to Jesus' natural human shrinking
from a painful death is clean contrary to the tendency to
underline his exaltation and majesty, and the portrait of
his disciples is quite unflattering. The whole has the
unmistakable ring of truth.

Prayer.

'And going a little farther, he fell on the ground and
prayed that, if it were possible, the hour might pass from
him' (14:35): his anxiety is expressed not only in words
but in action. The imperfect tense in the Greek indicates
prolonged prayer — he prayed and prayed. Of outstanding
interest is the idea of the appointed time, 'the hour' (cf
v. 41; 1:15; 13:32) — the moment chosen by God for the
fulfillment of his messianic destiny. The saying is strongly
reminiscent of Jn. 12:23: 'The hour has come for the Son
of man to be glorified'. In Mk. 14:36 we have Jesus'
prayer in direct speech. Mark shows a tendency to make a

statement about Jesus' teaching activity and follow it up immediately with direct discourse. This Gethsemane prayer is a striking case in point: 'he prayed that, if it were possible, the hour might pass from him. And he said, "Abba, Father, all things are possible to thee; remove this cup from me..." ' (14:35f). This is a progression from a first description of the content of the prayer and prepares the reader for the full impact of v. 36. In the prayer directly addressed to the Father the word 'hour' is replaced by that of 'cup', a biblical word to indicate a trial, a painful destiny. Better than in Lk. 22:42b Jesus' acceptance of the divine purpose is expressed by Mark: 'not what I will, but what thou wilt' (v. 36). In the Johannine scene so parallel to the agony in the garden (Jn. 12:27-29) we find again the stark humanity of Jesus. If in the agony he struggles with the human wish that the cup of suffering may pass him by, in John he struggles with his urge to cry 'Mercy! ' But he triumphs in each case by submitting to the Father's purpose. His prayer, 'Father, glorify thy name' (12:28) *is* his acceptance, for the name entrusted by the Father to Jesus (17:11f) is glorified only through the death, resurrection, and ascension of its bearer.

Watch and Pray.

The admonition to 'Watch' (Mk. 14:38), which is the theme of several of the parables of Jesus, was stressed in the early catechesis. Here the disciples are urged to 'watch and pray' lest they 'enter into temptation'. Jesus is referring to that trial of the disciples which will consist in the sight of their Lord handed over to an ignominious death: how could they still believe in him and his mission? But the 'temptation' is, too, the great eschatological trial. Jesus first passes through this trial, and all Christians must follow him. At his hour of trial Jesus chooses to drink the cup, he chooses the cross; his disciples must pray that they too, in their turn, will make the right choice. This is all the more needful in face of human frailty: 'the flesh is

weak'. The hour has indeed come: the betrayer is at hand
(Mk. 14:42) — it is too late for sleeping, or watching, or
praying.

He prayed more earnestly.

Matthew (26:36-46) adds little to Mark's narrative, but
Luke (22:39-46) has made his own important contribution. In his presentation Jesus does not look for human
comfort; instead, by his repeated warnings (vv. 40,46), *he*
seeks to fortify his disciples — rather than seek comfort
from them. It is an 'angel from heaven', that is, divine
help, which strengthens Jesus from his hour of death.
Already we have a notable step towards the Johannine
Jesus. 'And being in an agony he prayed more earnestly;
and his sweat became like great drops of blood falling
down upon the ground' (22:44). Like the previous verse,
referring to the angel, this verse, too, is proper to Luke.
It is not difficult to appreciate why both have been
omitted from some manuscripts of Luke, even from important Greek manuscripts. Clearly, the representation of
the Lord strengthened by an angel and the portrayal of
the painfully human details of the agony were too much
for some copyists; for the same reason it is inconceivable
that the verses could be a later insertion.

Comfort.

We should be thankful for this intimate glimpse into
the soul of Jesus. The ministration of an angel symbolizes
God's compassion for his Son and his answer to that
Son's prayer (cf Heb. 5:7). Throughout his gospel Luke
has drawn attention to the prayer of Jesus, and here is
the culmination: in anguish, vividly foreseeing and hu-
manly shrinking from, the horror of the passion, bur-
dened, above all, by his love for his own people and for
all men, he prayed more earnestly. He himself, in this
trial, this 'temptation', puts into practice his own recom-
mendation to his disciples. If Paul could understand so
clearly that the power of God can support our weakness

(cf 2 Cor. 12:10; Phil. 4:13), Jesus himself has experienced, with a clarity we cannot imagine, that weakness and that strength. This whole passage on the agony of our Savior should not only remind us of the cost of our redemption but, above all, should be a powerful encouragement to us. For indeed, our High Priest is no stranger to suffering; he knows the demands it makes on our human frailty and he can fully sympathize with our human lot (cf Heb. 4:15; 5:7-9).

In the garden, Jesus needed to have the assurance that what *seemed* to be asked of him really *was* asked of him. He sought that assurance in prayer. Once he was assured of the Father's will he found peace. We must not be misled by the angels of Luke. Always they are symbols, no more, of divine concern, of God's action. The 'angel from heaven' that strengthened Jesus was the strong help of the Father, experienced in prayer.

The Arrest.

With the arrest of Jesus the passion-narrative proper begins. The hour of the Son of man has come. Already his cup is overflowing: his betrayal is signaled by a friend's token of friendship (Lk. 22:48). While the synoptists give the impression that Judas had led a rabble to the garden, John (18:3,12) specifies that he simply guided a detachment of Roman soldiers and Temple police to the place where he knew Jesus was to be found. The story of the impulsive bystander who struck the high priest's servant is loosely attached to Mark's account (Mk. 14:47); it is more in place in Luke's setting (Lk. 22:49-50). One of the disciples struck off the man's ear — the right ear, thus inflicting greater dishonor (cf Mt. 5:39). John (18:10) tells us that the disciple was Simon Peter and that the slave was named Malchus. The healing of the man's ear, recounted by Luke only (22:51), was a gesture that this evangelist could not overlook. 'But this is your hour and the power of darkness' (Lk. 22:53). Jesus points out that now only, and not earlier, could his enemies have laid hands on him. God had willed that this should be their hour — or, rather, the hour of the prince of darkness whose instruments, like Judas, they were. Now is the 'appointed time' (4:13) and Satan had launched his final attack on Jesus. Then all the disciples forsook him and fled (Mk. 14:50; Mt. 26:56).

Master of his fate.

Matthew has underlined Jesus' complete control of the situation: 'Do you not think that I cannot appeal to my Father, and he will at once send me more than twelve legions of angels? (26:53). But it is John who has dramatized the situation. Already he is patently more interested in the symbolic value of Judas' going forth into the night than in his function of telling the authorities where Jesus could be arrested. 'It was night', we read, when Judas went out from the Last Supper to betray Jesus (Jn. 13:30), the evil night of which Jesus had warned (11:10; 12:35); John has given us a dramatic confrontation between Jesus, the Light of the world, and the forces of darkness in which men stumble. The episode also shows us that, for John, Jesus is the master of his own fate: just as he had permitted Judas to leave the supper room to betray him, so too does he allow Judas and his forces to arrest him. 'No one takes my life from me: I lay it down of my own accord' (Jn. 10:18). He permits himself to be arrested in fulfillment of his Father's will — just as the synoptists portrayed his submission to the Father under the image of the 'chalice' in Gethsemane. Moreover, Jesus' identifying himself with the words 'I am he' (Jn. 18:6,8) has, on one level, the same function as the 'kiss' in the synoptic betrayal. However, the whole of John's gospel points to the fact that by this 'I AM' he indicates a divine name. Jesus' adversaries are prostrate on their faces before his majesty. Because of his divine name he has power over the forces of darkness.

"Pilate protested, 'Why? What crime has he committed?'
  They only shouted the louder, 'Crucify him!'
So Pilate, who wished to satisfy the crowd . . .
  after he had had Jesus scourged, handed him over
to be crucified" (Mk. 15:15).

THE SCOURGING OF JESUS.

'If I have spoken rightly, why do you strike me?'.

Though the Rosary sequence: Scourging — Crowning with Thorns, does follow that of the gospel text it seems, in fact, that the episodes occurred the other way about. We may, however take them in the traditional order, all the more since they are moments in a tense and crowded drama, and our purpose is to bring out the deep meaning of the Passion.

Annas.

After his arrest, Jesus was taken to Annas, father-in-law of Caiaphas, the high priest (Jn. 18:13); Then, following a brief interrogation by Annas, Jesus spent the rest of the night in the courtyard of Annas' house. Luke tells us that his guards — the Temple police — passed the time by mocking their prisoner. 'Now the men who were holding Jesus mocked him and beat him; they also blindfolded him and asked him, "Prophesy! Who is it that struck you?" And they spoke many other words against him, reviling him' (Lk. 22:63-65). The guards play a brutal version of a guessing game with their prisoner; mindful of the religious charges brought against him, they declare that this 'prophet' should find the game an easy one. Here Jesus is mocked by the Jews as a prophet, as he will be mocked by the Roman soldiers as a King.

The Sanhedrin.

Mark and Matthew speak of two sessions of the Sanhedrin (the supreme Jewish religious council whose main components were the chief priests and the scribes), one at night which they describe in some detail (Mk. 14:53, 55-64; Mt. 26:57,59-66), the other, which they mention briefly, in the early morning (Mk. 15:1; Mt. 27:1). Luke speaks of one session only, and places it in the morning (Lk. 22:66-71). During the night he has the denials by Peter and the mockery of Jesus by his guards. Mark/Matthew's presentation is frankly unlikely: an (illegal) night assembly of the Sanhedrin is hard to accept and it is difficult to believe that the members of the Sanhedrin, so conscious of their dignity, would, immediately after the trial of Jesus, have taken part in the crude mockery scene; in Luke this last is shown as the guard's way of passing the night. In short, it can scarcely be doubted that Luke owes his better arrangement to an excellent source. Comparison with John not only confirms the order of Luke but helps to explain the presentation of Mark/Matthew. Luke omits the interrogation before the high priest (Annas) but sets the mocking scene at the courtyard of his house where Jesus was held in custody until next morning. Mark/Matthew, on the other hand, speak of two sessions, because there were two sessions; but they have substituted for the private interrogation of Annas, held at night, the more formal interrogation before the Sanhedrin next morning. The discrepancy between Mark/Matthew and Luke/John is explained by this simple displacement — one that easily occurred in the oral tradition.

A more fundamental issue is: was there a *trial* of Jesus at all? John appears to reject a Sanhedrin trial, at least in the form presented by the synoptists: 'Pilate said to them: "Take him yourself and judge him by your own law".' (Jn. 18:31). These words are meaningless if Jesus had been tried and sentenced to death by the Sanhedrin, as the synoptists say. Besides, the basic data of the 'trial' before the Sanhedrin appear in Jn. 10:24-39, but in a debate between Jesus and 'the Jews' at the Feast of Dedication. For John, there was no 'trial of Jesus' by the Sanhedrin because it does seem that he knew that the 'trial' was, in fact, an unofficial interrogation. If one adopts the Johannine position must one admit that the synoptists have given a false picture of the true course of events? Not if we respect their intentions. They have systematized what John has told us. There was indeed a meeting of the Sanhedrin on the morning following Jesus' arrest, to determine the kind of case that was to be put before Pilate. Taking occasion of this fact, the synoptic tradition sought to 'historicize' the effective cause of Jesus' death: the mounting hostility of the Jewish leaders, especially of the chief priests. For, one can readily assume that the real instigators of Jesus' death were members of the priestly class (hence the emphasis on the word against the Temple), exasperated by Jesus' attitude to the cultic practices. The Pharisaic scribes would have readily joined forces with them because they were affronted by Jesus' determined anti-legalist stance.

The Romans.

Jesus' execution was carried out by Romans and in accordance with Roman law – the Sanhedrin had handed him over to the Roman authorities. There is no reason to doubt the accuracy of the declaration in Jn. 18:31 – 'It is not lawful for us to put any man to death'. Judea was a Roman province and the removal of power to pass capital sentence was universal Roman practice. There was, in fact, no formal Sanhedrin trial. We may, then, ignore objections to the historicity of the trial based on alleged irregularities; and the alleged irregularities, besides, are based on later rabbinical jurisprudence. Our concern must be the theological assertions of the evangelists. All four are agreed that the religious authorities, wanting to get rid of Jesus, prepared a charge against him, which was then presented to the Roman procurator. And they agree that he yielded to political blackmail. The general picture is entirely credible. What the evangelists made of it all in their understanding of Christ is what interests the Christian.

The Temple.

In Mark's narrative (14:55-64) the statement of the false witnesses (v. 58) and of Jesus (v. 62) emphasize that Jesus' claim to be the Messiah was the real cause of his condemnation and of his death. The charge against Jesus runs: 'We heard him say, "I will destroy this temple that is made with hands, and in three days I will build another, not made with hands".' The original saying of Jesus, properly understood, is positive; it is not a question of destroying (though this is how the Sanhedrin want to take it) but of reconstructing. It looks to a renewal, to the raising up of a temple 'not made by human hands', that is, to a new cult, a new religious era. Jn. 2:19-22 offers the best commentary. Jesus freely surrenders his body to destruction, but within three days he will deliver it again from death (Jn. 10:18). This explanation makes Jesus the 'place' where God is to be adored, the true 'house of God'. With him and in him the time of the worship of God 'in spirit and truth' (4:23) has dawned.

Son of Man.

Because of lack of agreement on the part of the suborned witnesses, the high priest has to insist on an answer from Jesus. He puts an incriminating question: 'Are you the Christ, the Son of the Blessed? ' (14:61). In his reply: 'I am; and you will see the Son of man sitting at the right hand of Power, and coming with the clouds of heaven' (v. 62), Jesus gives a nuance of capital importance to the words of the high priest. He is the Messiah indeed, but one in terms of Ps. 110 and Dan. 7:13 – a heavenly messiah. What he says is: you will see the triumph of the Son of Man, crowned by God, placed at God's right hand. He speaks of his vindication, through resurrection. In Mark's intent, the vv. 61f have a further significance for his readers. Here we find, side by side, the two titles that recur in the gospel. Jesus has been singled out as Son of God in the voice from heaven at Baptism and Transfiguration and in the cries of the demons. He has been hailed as Messiah in Peter's confession at Caesarea Philippi and at the entry into Jerusalem. Now Mark brings these two titles together. In his view, the true character of Jesus expressed in these two terms is the reason why he was put to death.

Matthew's version (26:57-66) is much the same as Mark's. He does, however, assert that two witnesses were found whose evidence was precise (vv. 60f) — in contrast to Mark's yet not even so did their testimony agree' (Mk. 14:59). Matthew, too, has the high priest question Jesus with solemn formality: 'I adjure you by the living God' (v. 63); Jesus was constrained to reply. Perhaps the reason for Matthew's formulation is to explain Jesus' reply in this one case against his otherwise total silence (v. 63; 27:12,14) — a silence in fulfillment of Scripture (Is. 53:7). In Matthew, as in Mark, Jesus is asked if he is 'the Christ the Son of God'. Luke has separated the two titles: 'If you are the Christ, tell us' (22:67) and 'Are you the Son of God, then?' (v. 70) — so reflecting the fuller christian meaning of 'Son of God'. The evangelist has a similar gradation in his infancy gospel (1:21-33 and 1:35) as we have observed.

Son of God.

In our present passage the question of v. 67a regards the messianic status of Jesus. The first part of his reply, 'If I tell you, you will not believe', proper to Luke, is Johannine in tone (cf Jn. 10:25, which comes after a similar question). 'But from now on the Son of man will be seated at the right hand of the power of God' (v. 69). Luke avoids saying that the Sanhedrites 'will see' the Son of man or that he will 'come with the clouds of heaven' (Mk. 14:62; cf Dan. 7:13), apparently to avoid possible misunderstanding. In Dan. 7:13 the Son of man is borne on 'the clouds of heaven' into the divine presence; Mark applies the image to the triumphal return of the risen Christ to his Father — this the Sanhedrites 'will see'. But later, in certain christian milieux at least, this 'coming on clouds' was applied to the Parousia (cf 1 Thes. 4:16f); Luke does not wish his readers to believe (mistakenly) that Jesus had announced his imminent Parousia. But he does declare that 'from now on' the Son of man is exalted to the right hand of God (Ps. 110:1) because his imminent death is his entry into glory (cf Lk. 24:26; Acts 2:36). Jesus is the Messiah but, seated at the right hand of God, a Messiah of divine rank.

The second question of the high priest (v. 70) seeks to clarify this point: 'Are you the Son of God, then?' Though Luke does not use the term 'blasphemy' (cf Mk. 14:64), the reaction of the Sanhedrites shows that they consider Jesus guilty of that crime: he, a man, had 'made himself the Son of God' (Jn. 19:7). More clearly than Mark/Matthew, Luke has brought out the reason why Jesus was condemned to death. If he does not mention the sentence it may be because it had to be ratified by the Roman authorities; or, quite likely, because, like John, he was aware that the appearance of Jesus before the Sanhedrin was not in fact a trial at all. But the Sanhedrites had rejected, and had encompassed the death of, God's last messenger (19:44), their Messiah.

The Prophet.

The tradition of the mocking and maltreatment of Jesus is firm and well attested. It is represented in independent accounts: Mark/Matthew, Luke, and John. A pattern emerges from the different accounts: 1) Jesus is mocked as prophet and as king; 2) Jesus is mocked by the temple police, by Herod's soldiers, and by Roman soldiers. It would seem, too, that, for our purpose, the mocking of Jesus as prophet fits into the context of the

Scourging while the mockery of him as king will fit in the setting of the Crowning with Thorns.

We have already referred to the brutal treatment of Jesus by the temple police during his overnight custody in the courtyard of Annas' house (Lk. 22:63-65). In Mark 14:65 a brief account of the ill usage of Jesus is appended to the story of the Sanhedrin 'trial', and is manifestly a separate item of tradition. It is only the present position of the verse in Mark's gospel that would suggest that the 'some' who mocked Jesus ('And some began to spit on him, and to cover his face, and to strike him, saying to him, "Prophesy! " ' v. 65a) are members of the Sanhedrin. The second part of the verse ('and the guards received him with blows') would point to the more credible setting of Luke.

Yet again, the fourth evangelist may have given us the historical basis of the accounts of the maltreatment of Jesus. He tells us that when being interrogated by the high priest, Jesus was given a slap on the face by an officious policeman who took exception to his reply to a question: 'One of the Officers standing by struck Jesus with his hand, saying, "Is that how you answer the high priest? " ' (18:22) – there is the interesting Pauline parallel in Acts 23:1f. Jesus' reply underlines the injustice of this blow and of all the blows he was to suffer: 'If I have spoken wrongly, bear witness to the wrong; but if I have spoken rightly, why do you strike me? ' (Jn. 18:23). It seems very likely that it is the recollection of this incident, merged with Jesus' being mocked as a prophet by Jewish police in Annas' courtyard, that has given rise to Mark and Matthew's mockery scenes. This further elaboration has a theological motive – it fits in with the theme that Jesus died as the Suffering Servant: 'I gave my back to the smiters, and my cheek to those who pulled out the beard; I hid not my face from shame and spitting' (Is. 50:6; cf 53:3-5).

"*Weaving a crown of thorns they fixed it on his head, and stuck a reed in his right hand.*
Then they began to mock him by dropping to their knees before him, saying, 'All hail, king of the Jews!'" (Mt. 27:29).

THE CROWNING WITH THORNS.

'My kingship is not from the world'.

Our concern has been, following that of the evangelists themselves, as far as possible to bring out the theological significance of the gospel events. And that is why, at this point, we let St. John take over. Already we have noted his interpretation of the underlying features in the episode of the arrest of Jesus. We find that his narrative of the Trial of Jesus is markedly theological.

The Drama.

John presents the Passion as the triumph of the Son of God. The *dramatis personae* are sharply characterized.

Jesus: Despite appearances, he is always in control. He is the Judge who judges his judge (Pilate) and his accusers ('the Jews'). He is the King who reigns, with the cross as his throne – 'I, when I am lifted up from the earth, will draw all men to myself'.

The Jews: Not the whole Jewish people but its leaders who see Jesus as a danger to them, to the Establishment, and who are determined to destroy him. Before Pilate, they cast their charges in political terms: Jesus is a self-styled king, a rebel against Roman authority. They bring political pressure to bear on Pilate.

Pilate: He recognizes, and three times acknowledges, the innocence of Jesus. He desperately tries to compromise but ends by yielding to political blackmail. He is a man who will not make a decision for or against Jesus — and finds himself trapped.

Jesus before Pilate (Jn. 18:28 — 19:16a).

In the account of the trial we have present, in marked degree, a characteristic feature of the Fourth Gospel: narrative and discourse shaped by John with theological and dramatic concern, around a nucleus of historical tradition. Comparison with the earliest gospel is illuminating. In Mark, the account of the trial is very simple and consists of three episodes: 1) Jesus is brought to Pilate to be questioned about his claim to be king but refuses to answer; 2) Pilate offers Jesus to the crowd in place of Barabbas; 3) at the insistence of the crowd Pilate hands Jesus over to be crucified. Only at this point is Jesus taken inside the praetorium to suffer mockery. The trial itself had taken place in one outdoor setting. By contrast, the Johannine scenario is involved and dramatic. Now there are two stage settings: the *outer court* of the praetorium, where the Jews are gathered, is turbulent with frenzied shouts of hate as they put pressure on Pilate to find Jesus guilty. *Within the praetorium*, where Jesus is held prisoner, is an atmosphere of calm reason in which the innocence of Jesus becomes clearer to Pilate. In seven carefully balanced episodes arranged in a chiastic pattern, Pilate passes back and forth from one setting to the other, his movement giving external expression to the struggle taking place within him. The more convinced he becomes of Jesus' innocence, the more does political pressure build up to force him to condemn Jesus.

This careful literary structure of the Johannine account of the trial raises the question of its historicity. It may be said that, despite its drama and theology, John's account is really the most consistent and intelligible of all the gospels. The synoptic accounts of the trial before Pilate tell us little, whereas John's reconstruction does bring out the significance of it. Only John makes clear why Jesus was brought to Pilate in the first place and why Pilate gave in to having him crucified. Only John shows the interplay of subtle (and not so subtle) political forces on Pilate and indicates how Pilate's original questioning of Jesus concerned a political charge made against him. But this is not to say that John has given a totally different picture: he gives a more complete one.

King of the Jews.

Mark, we now realize, has given the key to the trial in the title 'King of the Jews' (15:2); thereafter he stresses that it is as King of the Jews (Messiah) that Jesus is rejected by the crowd and crucified (15:9,12,18,26,32). Luke, too, is aware that if Jesus were to be condemned by Pilate, the charge against him would have to be a political one, not a religious issue. In fact, the accusation against Jesus is threefold (Lk. 23:2): he has disturbed and stirred up the people; more specifically, he has forbidden the payment of tribute to Caesar; and he has put himself forward as the Messiah-King and so as a rebel against Roman authority. Pilate's reaction to the enigmatic reply of Jesus (23:3f) presupposes a longer interrogation similar to that in Jn. 18:35-38. Luke emphasizes Pilate's testimony to the innocence of Jesus: the procurator three times (as in John) declares his conviction that the prisoner is no criminal and offers no threat to Roman rule (Lk. 23:4,14,22). The Johannine account carries more detail than that of Luke and displays greater art, but it tells the same story.

Pilate.

There is indeed a theological reason for John's stress on the Roman trial. We are to see Pilate in the light of the rest of the Fourth Gospel. He provides yet another example of a reaction to Jesus which is neither faith nor rejection: the typical attitude of those who try to main-

tain a middle position in an all-or-nothing situation. In Jn.
4 the Samaritan woman was a person who, despite her
attempts to escape decision, yet could be led to believe in
Jesus. Pilate's refusal to make a decision for or against the
Light leads to tragedy. After he had assured Pilate that he
does not constitute a political danger because his 'kingship is not of this world' (18:36), Jesus goes on to challenge him to recognize the truth (v. 37): 'Everyone who is
of the truth hears my voice'. Because Pilate will not face
the challenge of deciding for the Truth in Jesus and
against the Jews, he thinks he can persuade the Jews to
accept a solution that will make it unnecessary for him to
decide for Jesus. This is the Johannine view of the episodes of Barabbas, the scourging, and the delivery of
Jesus to the Jews as 'your King'. For John, this trial is
our own tragic history of temporizing and indecision.
Pilate, the would-be neutral man is frustrated by the
presence of others outside of him. He failed to listen to
the truth and decide in its favor. He, and all who would
follow him, inevitably end up enslaved to this world.

The Jews.

After our outline of the interplay of dramatic and
theological motives in the Johannine account of the trial
before Pilate, we can do no more than look briefly at the
episodes within the trial scene. In the first episode
(18:28-32) the Jewish authorities ask Pilate to condemn
Jesus. 'The Jews' indicate to Pilate that they are accusing
Jesus of a capital civil offense — that Jesus is a revolu-
tionary with monarchical pretensions. They say that *they*
are not permitted to put anyone to death — a reference
to the fact that crucifixion is a Roman, not a Jewish,
punishment. But, in John's theology, their own plan to
kill him prevails: they had already determined that 'it is
more expedient for one man to die than that the whole
nation should perish' (Jn. 11:50). The irony is that they
did not know what they said. They intended to put Jesus
to death in order to prevent all men from coming to

believe in him, whereas in reality their 'lifting him up' on the Cross will be that which will draw all men to him.

Kingship.

In the second episode (18:33-38a) Pilate questions Jesus about his Kingship. The material is built around the question: 'Are you "the king of the Jews"? ' as John gives a splendid exposition of Jesus' Kingship. His Kingship belongs to the realm of Spirit, not flesh. He does not refuse to be known as 'King', but he prefers to describe his role in terms of testifying to the Truth. Indeed, in the whole of John, Jesus is portrayed not so much as a preacher of the Kingdom as a Revealer of the Truth. This is the real reason why he has been handed over to Pilate. The accused asks questions as if he were the judge and from his first words it is Pilate who is on trial. The subject of the trial is not whether Jesus is innocent or guilty (since Pilate proclaims him not guilty, v. 38b), but whether or not Pilate will respond to the truth. Pilate neither accepts the charges of the Jews nor listens to Jesus' voice. His asking 'What is truth? ' is John's way of showing that he has turned away from the truth, not recognizing it.

Barabbas.

In the third episode (18:38b-40) Pilate seeks to release Jesus, but the Jews choose Barabbas. Though John's account of the Barabbas incident is sketchy (compare Mk. 15:6-11) he makes it serve his interest by showing it as a travesty of justice. The indecisive Pilate cannot give Jesus justice after declaring him innocent, but he then releases one who really is guilty. Weakened by his failure to decide, Pilate is reduced from a position in which he could have ordered the freeing of Jesus to a position where he must bargain for it.

Scourging.

The fourth episode (19:1-3) combines two elements which are distinct: the scourging of Jesus and the

mocking of him as king. Scourging was the normal pre-
lude to crucifixion and is so presented, after sentence was
passed, in Mk. 15:15 and Mt. 27:26; Jesus was mocked
twice: by Temple police, as a prophet, in the courtyard
of Annas' house, and by roman soldiers, as a king (Mk.
15:16-20; Mt. 27:27-31), just before they led him off to
execution. John is right in associating scourging and (second) mockery, but he has situated them in the middle of
the trial as part of Pilate's benevolent plan (his sense of
justice has become warped) to release Jesus. In Roman
soldiers hailing Jesus as 'King of the Jews' we have an
example of Johannine irony. The protagonists are, unwittingly, declaring that the Gentiles will come to confess
the Kingship of Jesus.

Behold the Man.

The fifth episode (19:4-8) has Pilate presenting Jesus
to his own people, who clamor for his crucifixion. The
only feature of the scene shared with the synoptists is the
cry 'Crucify him! '. John develops the theme of Jesus'
Kingship: acknowledged by Pilate as the 'King of the
Jews', crowned and invested by the soldiers, Jesus now
undergoes another ceremony in the coronation ritual. He
is brought out, clad in royal purple, crowned and with a
scepter in his hand, to receive the acclamation of his
people. The expression, 'Behold the man! ', meant in con-
temptuous derision, becomes in John an exalted title
voicing the ironic fulfillment of Israel's long wait for her
messianic King. In this episode we meet the real motive
behind the Jews' desire to kill Jesus: 'He has made himself the Son of God'. In the sixth episode (19:9-11) Pilate
talks with Jesus about power. As when he had earlier
asked Jesus about kingship (episode 2), Pilate asks questions on one level, whereas Jesus answers on another.
Moreover, each time Pilate's first question gets him nowhere; only the second elicits Jesus' answer. Again Jesus
affirms that no one can take his life from him (cf
10:17f): he voluntarily enters the hour appointed by his

Father. This is the only reason that Pilate has any power over him: God has assigned to Pilate a certain role in Jesus' 'hour'.

Delivered up.

Truly, God has planned this hour carefully as the seventh and final episode conveys (19:12-16). Pilate yields to the Jewish demand for Jesus' crucifixion. John's account of the passing of sentence of death is detailed, dramatic, and theological; the only points of parallel with the synoptics are in the repeated cry for crucifixion and the outcome of Jesus' being 'handed over'. The Old Testament background to this verb used by all the evangelists, implies that Jesus was 'delivered up' by 'the definite plan and foreknowledge of God' (Acts 2:23). The real trial is over when the Jews utter the fateful words, 'We have no king but Caesar! '. This is akin to the statement in Matthew's account: 'His blood be upon us and upon our children' (Mt. 27:25). Both evangelists are reflecting not history but apologetic theology. The tragedy of Jesus' death became seen through the hostility between Church and Synagogue in the late first century A.D. The audience at the trial are made to voice a christian interpretation of salvation history.

The Lamb.

John also tells us that it was noon of Passover Eve when the fatal renunciation of the Messiah was voiced. This was the hour when the Passover lambs had begun to be sacrified in the Temple. It is supreme Johannine irony: the Jews renounce the covenant at the very moment when the priests begin to prepare for the Feast which annually recalled God's deliverance of his covenanted people. By the blood of a lamb in Egypt Yahweh had marked them off to be spared as his own. Now, they know no king but the emperor, and they slay another Lamb. At this moment, just before the Passover, as Jesus set out for Golgotha to shed his saving blood, the trial of

Jesus ends with the fulfillment of that prophecy at the
beginning of the gospel: 'Behold the lamb of God who
takes away the sin of the world! ' (Jn. 1:29).

"As they led him away, they laid hold of one Simon,
the Cyrenean who was coming in from the fields.
They put a crossbeam on Simon's shoulder for him
to carry along behind Jesus" (Lk. 23:26).

THE WAY OF THE CROSS.

'He went out, bearing his own cross'.

'And they led him out to crucify him' (Mk. 15:20b). The evangelists display a reticence in regard to the details of the crucifixion that later christian tradition would have done well to imitate. One cannot help reflecting that in much pietistic reflection on the sufferings and death of Jesus there has been an unhealthy element, a masochistic trend. The evangelists do not veil the grim reality but they certainly do not linger morbidly over the details. There have been more horrible deaths than that of Jesus. The decisive factor was that he accepted his death voluntarily, and his death was transformed by resurrection. The true human attitude to suffering, both in anticipation (Gethsemane) and in the enduring of it (Calvary) is that of *the* Man, and not in the 'experience' of ascetics and martyrs beloved of hagiographers.

For the details of the Way of the Cross we turn to Luke and John, for they have filled out the laconic statements of Mark (15:21) and Matthew (27:32), and have done so distinctively: we find here the sensitivity of Luke and the dramatic theology of John.

The Road to Calvary (Lk. 23:26-32).

Jesus was led away by Roman soldiers. Simon 'who was coming in from the country' as the grim cortege went

on its way was a Jew of the Diaspora, from Cyrene in
North Africa, but now living in Jerusalem. Luke omits the
Marcan detail that he was 'the father of Alexander and
Rufus' (Mk. 15:21) — doubtless Christians known to
Mark's community. Luke's phrasing, '[they] laid on him
the cross, to carry it behind Jesus' in a conscious echo of
the saying, 'Whoever does not bear his own cross and
come after me, cannot be my disciple' (14:27). He has
presented Simon as the model of the Christian who walks
in the footsteps of his Master. The rest of this passage is
proper to Luke.

These women who followed the three condemned men
are not the Galilean women mentioned in 8:2f; they are,
perhaps, women who had known Jesus or women who
habitually attended to the last needs of condemned criminals, and who prepared the spiced wine. One of the many
meeting places of Luke and John is their insistence on
Jesus' concern for and relation to womenfolk. Luke's
discernment is well known, but it is John who has told
us: 'Now Jesus *loved* Martha and her sister and Lazarus'
(11:5). It is salutary that the evangelists stress the role of
women in the Passion. Where men failed lamentably,
women alone showed compassion and fidelity. Luke mentions the presence of two criminals who were to be
executed with Jesus (in the other gospels they emerge
more abruptly) for one of them plays an important role
in his narrative of the crucifixion.

Enthronement.

In the Johannine account of the death of Jesus
(19:17-42) the kingship motif is continued. Jesus goes
forth to Calvary in triumphal procession, bearing his own
cross, the instrument of his victory. In the episode of the
Royal Inscription (19:19-22) John presents the crucifixion as Jesus' enthronement. All the gospels agree that
the charge of being a royal pretender was inscribed
against Jesus. But John has turned it into a worldwide
proclamation: 'and it was written in Hebrew, in Latin,

and in Greek'. Pilate's heraldic inscription, and his firm refusal to change it, shows Jesus formally acknowledged as King by the greatest political power on earth. The cross is where this king is enthroned: 'I, when I am lifted up from the earth, will draw all men to myself'. Ironically, the Gentiles acknowledged what the Jews would seek to deny.

THEOLOGY OF THE CROSS.

John's theological concern prompts us to look to the theology of the cross. We turn to Mark and, more briefly, to Paul. Suffering plays such a large place in Mark's gospel that it has often been called a 'Passion Narrative with an Introduction'. Mark gives his answer to the 'why' of the scandal of the cross, of the Son of God's having died a criminal's death at the hands of the highest religious and political authorities.

The Suffering Messiah.

The central importance of Peter's confession: 'You are the Christ' (8:29) at a turning-point in Mark's gospel is indicated by the brusque change of tone and of orientation after Peter has acknowledged the messiahship of Jesus. In the actual structure of the gospel the prediction of the Passion (8:31-32a) is Jesus' response to the confession of Peter, and the evangelist sees an intimate link between this first prediction and Peter's confession. The following section of Mark's gospel (8:31 – 11:10) is dominated by the prophecies of the passion (8:31; 9:12; 9:31; 10:33f); and the violent protestation of Peter in 8:32 ('And Peter took him, and began to rebuke him') shows clearly that this is a new and unexpected teaching. 'And he said this plainly' (8:32a) – it is indeed a turning-point in the self-revelation of Jesus: until now he has said nothing explicitly about his messiahship. But now he speaks to the disciples quite plainly of his destiny of suffering and death.

Scandal of the Cross.

'And Peter took him and began to rebuke him'
(v. 32b). The idea of a suffering Messiah was entirely
foreign to Peter; despite his confession he had not grasped
the essential meaning of discipleship. In his surprise and
his upset at the unexpected prospect he dares to 'rebuke'
Jesus — something that no other disciple had ever done.
In his turn Jesus rebuked Peter: 'Get behind me, Satan! '
— the words recall Mt. 4:10, 'Begone, Satan'. The temptation in the wilderness (Mt. 4:1-11; Lk. 4:1-13) aimed at
getting Jesus himself to conform to the popularly accepted messianic role, to become a political messiah. It
was an attempt to undermine his full acceptance of the
will of God; here Peter plays Satan's role. Peter's acknowledgment of Jesus as Messiah had set him and the
disciples apart from 'men' (v. 27); but now Peter is rebuked for thinking as men think. Peter, and all like him,
who stand 'on the side of men', stand opposed to God's
saving purpose and align themselves with Satan.

Disciples.

Thus, we find that the passage is concerned not
primarily with the historical situation of the ministry of
Jesus, but with the historical situation of the church for
which Mark is writing. The reply to Jesus' first question
refers to opinions available in the Palestinian situation of
the ministry (v. 28); in the reply to the second question,
the title 'Christ' has christian overtones, and the prediction of the Passion is cast in language of the early Church
(vv. 29,31). Peter's reaction and the sharp correction of it
(vv. 32f) have much to do with an understanding of
christology. Historically, Jesus and Peter engage in dialogue. At a deeper level, 'Jesus' is the Lord addressing his
Church and 'Peter' represents fallible believers who confess correctly, but then interpret their confession incor-
rectly. Similarly, the 'multitude' (v. 34) is the people of
God for whom the general teaching (8:34 — 9:1) is

meant. A story about Jesus and his disciples has a further purpose in terms of the risen Lord and his Church.

Here, then, more obviously than elsewhere, Mark is writing for his community. Here, above all, he is concerned with christology. The confession of Peter is the facile profession of too many of Mark's contemporaries: 'You are the Christ'. Everything depends on what they mean by that profession and its influence on their lives. They cannot have a risen Lord without a suffering Messiah; they cannot be disciples without walking his road of suffering. Mark's admonition here is quite like that of Paul: 'When we cry "Abba! " "Father! " it is the Spirit himself bearing witness with our spirit that we are children of God, and if children then heirs, heirs of God and fellow workers with Christ, *provided we suffer with him* in order that we may be glorified with him' (Rom. 8:15-17).

Foolishness of the Cross.

For Mark, the problem of a suffering Messiah is the mystery of a messianic history which takes the form of a passion history. 'The Son of man must suffer many things' — the messianic story is no uninterrupted success story; it is a story of suffering, rejection, failure. This fact must influence and color all we say about life and salvation. Jesus immediately runs into opposition: 'Peter. . . began to rebuke him'. Quite obviously, Peter has spoken for all of us. Jesus confirms this: 'You are on the side of men' — you think the thoughts of man. Not the thoughts of the arrogant, the proud, but the natural reaction of those who shrink from a way of suffering. Have we, at bottom, any different idea of salvation from that of Peter? Can we really conceive salvation other than in categories of victory? We experience the saying of Jesus again and again as contradiction, we cannot reconcile ourselves to it. The rebuke of Jesus did not change Peter: he will deny the suffering Messiah. The other disciples will sleep and will abandon him. And the Church, which

began with the apostles who failed to understand will,
time and again, like them, fail to understand.

The Church must resist the temptation to re-interpret
the scene, to turn it, somehow, into one of triumph. The
Church must never forget the extent to which it owes its
existence not to a conqueror but to one vanquished, not
to one who overcame but to one who was overcome. It
owes its life to one who was judged by the standards of
men: it is expedient that this man should die. And he was
condemned to death, and crucified.

The Lamb who was slain.

This, too, is a central lesson of the great Apocalypse of
John: that there is only *one* way to christian victory, one
christian triumph. Christ won his victory through suffering and death. 'They [the martyrs] have conquered him
[the Dragon] by the blood of the Lamb and by the word
of their testimony for they loved not their lives even unto
death' (Rev. 12:11). This is put even more poignantly in
chapter 13: 'If any one is to be taken captive, to cap-
tivity he goes; if any one slays with the sword, with the
sword must he be slain. Here is a call for the endurance
and faith of the saints' (13:10). The whole is a warning
against any attempt on the part of the Church to resist,
violently, its persecutors. If a Christian is condemned to
exile, as John had been, he is to regard exile as his al-
lotted portion, and to go readily; if he is sentenced to
death he is not to lift his hand against the tyrant; to do
so will be to deserve his punishment. It is precisely this
suffering without resistance which calls for patient endurance and faith. This is unpalatable teaching – it has about
it the foolishness of the Cross. But, the foolishness of the
Cross is the wisdom of God. How is a wrong put out of
commission? Certainly not by retaliation and not really
by retribution. Only if the victim absorbs the wrong and
puts it out of currency is it prevented from going any

further. The whole force of Evil was absorbed by the
silent suffering and boundless love of the Lamb who was
slain. This is the meaning of the word that follows the
prediction of suffering and death: '. . . and after three
days rise again'. These words are not meant to allay our
fears, not meant to soften the stark reality of suffering
and death. That word of the victory of the Son of Man
over death is a promise of victory for the oppressed, the
vanquished, the silent in death — the forgotten. It is a
word of warning against our human way of exalting the
victorious and triumphant. Through the suffering Messiah
victory is possessed by the vanquished; through the dead
Messiah life is possessed by the dead. He and his way are
the sole guarantee of our victory and of our life.

But 'let him who would follow me take up his cross
daily. . .' (Lk. 9:23). Discipleship, entry into the kingdom
which Jesus has brought in his person, includes suffering.
Proving one's discipleship means staying by Jesus in his
trials. However, because the disciple who 'takes up his
cross daily' is also a child of God, he will see suffering in
a new light. No longer does he ask 'why' God sends suffering, but 'for what'. When one is a child of God the
unfathomable riddle of evil is left in God's hands. Nothing
happens without our Father.

The Word of the Cross.
  There remains our constant temptation to distort the
theology of the Cross preached by Paul into a 'respect-
able' theology. The abidingly critical function of Pauline
(and Marcan) theology for the world is seen in the urgent
and unmistakable reference of the Apostle to the death
and resurrection of Christ as the fundamental and totally
decisive saving event which always brings to naught every
glorification of Church and world. For Paul insists on the
'scandalous' and 'foolish' 'word of the cross' which the
'wisdom of the world' can neither verify nor falsify (1

Cor. 1:18-25). But this word is, too, a word of hope. Because of its close link with the kerygma of the resurrection it is a word which opens up a future to all mankind, as it looks beyond the boundaries of death and leads men beyond death.

"Near the cross of Jesus there stood his mother . . .
Seeing his mother there with the disciple whom he
loved, Jesus said to his mother, 'Woman, there is your
son.' And in turn he said to the disciple, 'There is
your mother'" (John 19:26-27).

THE CRUCIFIXION AND DEATH OF JESUS.

'Woman, behold your son! '.

Jesus was led to the place of death. It was Jewish custom, inspired by Prov. 31:6, to offer wine drugged with myrrh to the condemned. Jesus would not drink, but willed to undergo his sufferings in full consciousness. 'And they crucified him': the dread deed is recorded in the simplest possible terms. There is no description of the crucifixion. For the earliest tradition, and for the evangelists, crucifixion was a horrible and degrading contemporary method of execution; there was nothing at all glamorous about it. They had no yearning to linger over the grim details. Perhaps christian piety woud have been well advised to have imitated their reticence. What the evangelists proceed with, right away, is the interpretation of the death of Jesus.

Forgiveness.

Jesus was not crucified alone: two others, 'robbers', that is rebels like Barabbas, were crucified with him. The inscription, or title, is in accordance with Roman custom. 'The King of the Jews': underlining the fact that Jesus was executed as *Messiah*. Jesus is the one who saves men; that is why he dies. Luke alone (23:34) — 'And Jesus said, "Father, forgive them; for they do not know what they do" ' — records the moving prayer of forgiveness.

The omission of the saying by a goodly number of manuscripts can be explained on the grounds of its apparently
excessive indulgence towards the Jews and its seeming
contradiction of other sayings. These words of forgiveness
are not primarily for the soldiers, who are merely carrying
out orders, but for the Jewish leaders. They cannot be
absolved from guilt in their calculated rejection of Jesus
and in the manner in which they engineered his death.
But they were motivated by fierce zeal for their religion
(as Paul was to be) and they did sincerely believe Jesus
guilty of blasphemy. This prayer of Jesus is not only perfectly in character; it is the climax of his condescension,
so visible in the parables, towards these stubborn men.
The prayer of Stephen (Acts 7:60) is surely meant as an
intentional parallel.

The 'Good Thief'.

In place of the brief statement by Mark and Matthew
that the two crucified men also reviled Jesus, Luke
(23:39-43) declares that only one acted so. The other
acknowledged Jesus' innocence. In Luke's eyes these two
men symbolize Jews and Romans in their attitude to
Jesus. The former, like the Jews, seeks in Jesus a Messiah
who would arise in power and dramatically deliver Israel
— and rejects him when these hopes are dashed. The
other, like Pilate, admits that Jesus has done nothing
wrong, and does not deny his Kingship. Further, he recognizes Jesus as the Messiah. He asks to be remembered
when Jesus comes in his kingly power, that is, when he
comes to inaugurate the messianic age, an event which, in
Jewish belief, would involve the resurrection of the dead.
Jesus, the Savior, assures the 'good thief' that his prayer
will be answered more promptly than he could have
dreamed. This very day, after death, he will enter with
Jesus into the life of God; he will be with Christ in the
abode of happiness conjured up by the word Paradise.

Behold your Son.

The central episode in John's crucifixion scene is when

Jesus gives his mother Mary to the beloved disciple (19:25-27). The words of Jesus to those standing beneath him are like a revelatory formula: the sonship and motherhood proclaimed from the Cross are related to God's plan and Jesus' final accomplishment. It is only after this point that Jesus became aware that 'all was now accomplished' (v. 28). The action of Jesus in relation to his mother and the beloved disciple completes the work that the Father has given Jesus to do and fulfills the Scripture. Both here and at the scene in Cana she is called 'Woman'. But whereas there she was refused a role in Jesus' ministry, here she receives her role — at her Son's final hour of death. United to the redemptive sacrifice of her Son, in the travail of Calvary, she became again a mother. For, in pointing out to her the disciple who stood there (the 'beloved disciple', that is, the Christian): 'Woman, behold your son' — Jesus called her to a new, spiritual motherhood which will henceforth be hers towards the people of God. Jesus shows his concern for the community of believers now drawn to him as he is lifted up on the cross. Henceforth, the Mother of God is mother, too, of those other children of God, the brethren of her Son.

Desolation.

The three synoptists tell of cosmic phenomena and protentous happenings which accompanied the death of Jesus, such as darkness and the rending of the Temple veil; Matthew is the most elaborate and includes the resurrection of 'many of the saints'. We should realize that here the tradition has clothed the event in the imagery of the Day of Yahweh: to the eyes of the first Christian the day of Jesus' death is the day of God's judgment and the beginning of the eschatological age, and we are dealing here with conventional, symbolic language. The cry of Jesus: 'My God, my God, why have you forsaken me? ' is omitted by Luke and John. It is important to recognize that the cry is the opening verse of a psalm (Ps. 22)

which ends in an utterance of faith; the whole context of
the psalm must be kept in mind. Nonetheless, the distress
of Jesus was real: a deeply felt sense of desolation and
abandonment, so that, for a time, the closeness of Jesus'
communion with the Father was obscured. Here again, as
a Gethsemane, we see the stark humanity of Jesus. Never
was the distance between feeling and fact more amazingly
revealed. Jesus, at this awful moment, *felt* abandoned by
the Father; the fact was that, in this supreme expression
of his acceptance of the Father's will, this expression of
filial love, he was never closer to the Father. Truly, he is
like us in all things. Saints have borne witness that the
most faithful servants of God can experience these dark
moments when they have 'lost' God, only to recognize, in
retrospect, that God's love had touched them, most particularly, at those times.

Fulfillment.

The 'loud cry' of the dying Jesus is a conventional
phrase: though Mark suggests a sudden, violent death.
Luke gives as his dying prayer a psalm-text (Ps. 31:6),
'Father, into thy hands I commit my spirit'. 'He breathed
his last' — 'and they crucified him': the death of Jesus is
described as tersely and unemotionally as the deed of
nailing to the cross. There is no need to gloss these grim
facts. Yet, John does make his contribution. The last
word: 'It is fulfilled' is a cry of victory — now Jesus will
draw all men to himself. 'He gave up his spirit' (Jn.
19:30): Jesus dies, but his Spirit will take over his work
of drawing men to himself. Jesus is now glorified in the
completion of his hour, the fulfillment of God's purpose
— and so the Spirit now is given (cf 7:39).

Life from death.

The final episode, the breaking of Jesus' legs and the
flow of blood and water (Jn. 19:31-37) is the only part
of John's crucifixion narrative which has no parallel in

the synoptics. The beloved disciple speaks here as a witness vital for all Christians whom he symbolizes. In this
flow of water and blood from the side of Jesus, from
within him, John saw a fulfillment of Jesus' own promise:
' "Out of his heart shall flow rivers of living water". Now
this he said of the Spirit. . .' The flow of blood and water
is another proleptic reference to the giving of the Spirit.
On another, secondary, level this flow of blood, and
water symbolizes the sacraments of Eucharist and Baptism
and points to their source in Jesus; through these sacraments the life of Jesus is communicated to the Christian.
Blood and water flow from the *dead* Jesus. The drama of
the cross does not end in death but in a flow of life that
comes from death. The death of Jesus on the cross is the
beginning of christian life. Finally, reference to the Passover lamb of which 'not a bone could be broken' (Ex.
12:10,46) forms an inclusion with the 'Lamb of God'
heralded by the Baptist at the beginning of the gospel
(1:29).

The Son of God.

The rending of the Temple veil — the curtain which
hung in front of the Holy Place and shut off the interior
of the Temple from the view of those who stood in the
outer courts — is manifestly symbolical. The religion of
Israel, the cult of the true God, until now shut off (by
the veil) from the eyes of the Gentiles, is now open to
all: the veil is gone, the new religion is universalist, open
to all men. By his death Christ has opened the way, for
all, to the heavenly sanctuary (Heb. 10:19f). The centu-
rion who was in charge of the execution becomes another
witness to the innocence of Jesus: 'Certainly, this man
was innocent' (Lk. 23:47): he had seen in Jesus the perfect man whose martyr's death is a glory to God. But
Mark has: 'Truly this man was the Son of God! ' (15:39).
This public proclamation by a Gentile that Jesus was the
'Son of God' rounds off Mark's gospel and fulfills his
theological purpose. He had set out to write 'the gospel

of Jesus Christ, the Son of God' (1:1) and at this climactic moment he has the solemn confession of the
divine sonship of Jesus. It is the significance of Jesus'
death for the Gentile world.

THE GLORIOUS MYSTERIES

THE GLORIOUS MYSTERIES.

'. . . and enter into his glory?'.

Faith in the resurrection of Christ is the foundation-stone of the Church. But we must realize that this faith is not just belief in the historical fact that Jesus rose from the dead; it is faith in the deeper, spiritual meaning of the resurrection. We should understand that the apostolic preaching developed a theological interpretation of the fact of the resurrection. It is the Father's glorification of the Son, and thus sets the seal of God's approval on the redemptive event. By it Jesus is constituted 'Christ and Lord', 'Chief and Savior', 'Judge and Lord of living and dead'. Now at last the full meaning of his earthly life appears: he is the manifestation of God here below, of God's love and of his grace.

Exaltation to the right hand of the Father is another aspect of the resurrection: he is 'designated Son of God in power'. His messianic task is done, and he has completed his work as Messiah in the fullest sense by returning to the Father — thus deserving anew the name that was his from eternity: Son of God. And, returned to the Father, he can now send forth the Spirit. The risen Christ is the source of the new spiritual creation. He has power to transform into his image all who are united to him by faith; he communicates his life to Christians.

'God's love has been poured into our hearts through the Holy Spirit which has been given to us' (Rom. 5:5).

The Spirit of God, sent forth by Christ, makes us sons of God. He speaks to the heart of God's child and convinces him that he really is a child of God. And the Spirit inspires him to call God by the same familiar name that Jesus used: *Abba*. In doing so, the Spirit 'speaks what he hears' and 'takes what is of Jesus' and declares it, because it is the Son who has made us sons. The Christian, in being taught how to address his Father, learns of the confidence he should have in him. But we must act like children of a loving Father – we must be moved by love. If the Spirit does dwell within us, our whole conduct should be inspired by him: "If we live by the Spirit, let us also walk by the Spirit (Gal. 5:25).

Saint Paul has confidently asserted that 'we shall certainly be united with Christ in a resurrection like his' (Rom. 6:5). But we are human and need support and comfort in our hope for that future. We find it in the Assumption of Mary. We have the solemn assurance that one of our race does indeed live, here and now, the eternal life with Christ. In her we have the assurance that death, for us, is a going to the Lord. If the risen Christ is the cause of our resurrection, it is natural that the 'power of his resurrection' should be effective also here and now. And so it is. This fact offers an occasion for reflection on the signification of the Risen Lord in the life of Christians.

If we need hope for the future we need too confidence for the present. We find this in Mary's motherhood of us. For if Mary is Queen of Heaven it is that she may make intercession for her children on earth. We should never forget that it is the title Mother of God which defines Mary's function in the work of salvation: she must be seen always in relation to her Son. And Mary could not have been so closely united with the Saviour without in some way entering into his work, entering into the scheme of redemption. She takes her place within the saving plan of God, in dependence on her divine Son. Her motherly office exercized towards men in no way detracts from the unique mediation of Christ. She does not stand between the faithful and her Son; rather, her one intention is to bring about a direct union between Christ and his faithful. The mediating concern of Mary is that the faithful 'may cling the more closely to the Mediator and the Savior'.

"... go to my brothers and tell them,
   'I am ascending to my Father and your Father,
to my God and your God!'" (John 20:17).

THE RESURRECTION.

'The Lord has risen indeed! '

The crucifixion of Jesus is obviously an event on the historical plane. Yet, at the same time, and with more truth, it is an event on the spiritual plane; we have seen that John has consistently stressed this aspect of it. The resurrection, on the other hand, is first and foremost a reality on the spiritual plane, and the evangelists seek to show that it is also an event on the historical plane. This is the reason for the stress — particularly in Luke and John — on the reality of the post-resurrection appearances of Jesus and on his renewal of personal relations with the disciples. They show that the death-and-resurrection, while retaining its full spiritual significance, is of vital importance for men because it happened as a matter of history, at a point of time, in this world.

Resurrection.

The early Church saw the resurrection of Jesus as the divine confirmation of Jesus' mission. Because the disciples did not experience it as an 'event' in history but rather as belonging to the last age, Christ's rising from the dead is presented as a resurrection to *doxa* (glory) rather than as a return to earthly life. Through believing, the early community really experienced the dawning of God's new world, and this in turn gave birth to the Church. History, in the New Testament, is the expression of the meaning which the facts held for the Church's faith, which centred upon the Resurrection. It thus follows that the facts remembered about this event are recorded in the gospels as understood on the further side of Resurrection. Rather than a falsification, this is simply in keeping with the whole mystery implied by the Resurrection: only symbol and imagery, not literal prose, could tell *this* story. Something had happened to these men which they could describe only by saying that they had 'seen the Lord' – that the Lord had 'shown himself' to them. This phrase did not refer to some general christian experience but rather to a particular series of òccurrences confined to a limited period. Such occurrences, on the threshold of ordinary human experience, just would not submit to precision of detail. 'The original witnesses were *dead sure* that they had met with Jesus, and there was no more to be said about it' (C. H. Dodd).

The Father.

We find that, predominantly in the New Testament references to Jesus' resurrection, the Father is the author of his resurrection (Acts 2:24,32; 3:15,26; Rom. 8:11; Gal. 1:1; Col. 2:12). 'God raised Jesus from the dead' appears to be the oldest formulation of the Easter message. It expresses the conviction that Jesus of Nazareth has triumphed over death. But, as in other areas of christology, here too there is a development. At an intermediate stage it is said that Jesus 'has been raised' (1 Cor. 15:12-20). Paul, in this passage, is primarily proclaiming that Jesus is risen today; he is stressing the new condition of Christ. The important fact is the risen Christ, here and now, and not a past action of raising from the dead. Finally, in John, Jesus is the agent of his own resurrection: it is he who lays down his life and it is he who takes it up again (Jn. 2:19; 10:17).

Victor over Death.

But, however they expressed it, Christians were, from

the first, convinced that the crucified Jesus was not held by death. In Jewish faith and prayer God is he who 'makes the dead live'. Jewish faith and hope looked to a resurrection of the righteous, at the end of time. What the first Christians asserted was that, in the person of Jesus of Nazareth, this divine act had taken place. Jewish expectation was eschatological: resurrection was an event of the End-time. Christians asserted that an eschatological event had taken place in time. If one can put it so, the resurrection of Jesus is an event at once eschatological and historical. In essence, it is a spiritual event, beyond our world of time, and yet it has impinged on our world of time. Under its historical aspect, the resurrection can be set in a series of events: death, burial, resurrection, exaltation, ascension. We shall see that resurrection and exaltation are two aspects of a single mystery, while the ascension is a farewell, not a first return to the Father. Yet the 'historical' sequence is not devoid of meaning for how can time-bound man speak of realities beyond our world except in terms of our world?

The narratives.

Six gospel passages serve as sources for our knowledge of the Resurrection: Mk. 16:1-8; Mt. 28; Lk. 24:13-49; Jn. 20; Jn. 21; Mk. 16:9-20; and to these must be added Paul's text in 1 Cor. 15:5-8. In this group we may distinguish two types of narrative: those of the post-resurrection appearances and those of the finding of the empty tomb. The narratives of the post-resurrection appearances were composed first, to ground christian faith in the risen Jesus and to justify apostolic preaching. The very nature of such appearances make it obvious enough that the gospels cannot agree where and to whom Jesus appeared. This diversity does not seriously affect the historicity of the events but rather is a product of the way in which the stories were told and preserved. A basic pattern is followed when Jesus is said to appear to the Twelve (eleven): the disciples are together, and are somewhat apprehensive. Jesus appears, is at first unrecognized, and ends by giving a solemn command. This includes the commission to carry to men the good news of Jesus and his gift of salvation. Each gospel witness stresses some particular appearance or some significant aspect of one, and each evangelist has presented the material in the light of his own theological interest. We may think of Luke's memorable account of the appearance on the road to Emmaus, or John's moving picture of Jesus standing on the lake shore and inviting the disciples to have breakfast with him.

The tomb.

The narratives of the finding of the empty tomb have more uniformity. That the evangelists do differ in narratives of the appearances shows that the primitive narrative account did not contain such localized apparitions. That they agree in telling us that women followers of Jesus found the tomb empty on Sunday morning suggests that the story of burial in the primitive passion account was never the end of the story. There was always this indication that something lay beyond the grave. Thus, the claim that women (who in Jewish law had no value as witnesses) found the tomb of Jesus empty may go as far back as we can trace in the traditional proclamation of Jesus' resurrection.

He is not here.

We can look, now, to some specific contribution of each evangelist in his presentation of the resurrection. It is today more commonly agreed that the resurrection-narrative, abbreviated though it is, forms the conclusion of Mark's gospel (16:1-8) — with 16:9-20 as a later ending by another hand. He has seized the occasion of the finding of the empty tomb to proclaim, by the mouth of an angel, the resurrection message. Luke and John reflect more precisely the primitive resurrection tradition, for they portray how Mary Magdalene and Peter came and found the tomb empty, were perplexed, then illumined by an appearance of Jesus. Mark seems to reflect a second stage in the tradition. He mentions no apparition of Jesus; rather, an Easter message is connected with the finding of the empty tomb. Mark uses the *angelus interpres* ('angel spokesman') technique to give, at once (it is a kind of shorthand), the true explanation of the empty tomb. 'Do not be amazed; you seek Jesus of Nazareth, who was crucified. He has risen, he is not here. . .! ' (Mk. 16:6). Here is the kernel of the christian message. The original Marcan ending seems abrupt: we are left with women who have fled from the tomb, in fear and trembling, saying nothing to anyone. Yet we do have a perfectly suitable ending to a gospel. The point of Jesus' resurrection is made with all necessary emphasis. The reaction of the women expresses that awe and amazement which news of the resurrection must always arouse in those who really understand its import. Mark ended his book here and gave no account of an apparition of Jesus because, in his opinion, he had already said everything necessary. He had established the fact of the resurrection through the angel spokesman; he had also indirectly mentioned Jesus' appearance to the disciples by saying that Jesus would go before them into Galilee.

He showed himself.

In 1 Cor. 15 Paul uses the same verb *ōphthē* to state that Christ 'appeared' to Cephas, to James, and to Paul himself. The word can mean, and seemingly does mean, 'he showed himself'. It means that the risen Jesus manifested himself as present in some way, that he showed himself, so that Paul, or the others, can say: 'I have seen the Lord'. What is involved is a divine initiative leading to a real experience of the presence of the Lord and a firm conviction of the reality of this presence. More than that we cannot say, nothing about the exact manner of this experience. But what we have said is already much, and it is enough. We are in the realm of faith.

At the tomb.

As we have come to expect, the Johannine resurrection narrative too is dramatic. It divides into two scenes: 'at the tomb' (20:1-18) and 'where the disciples were gathered' (20:19-29). Each scene has a definite time setting at the beginning and in each there are two episodes: in the first, the disciples come to faith; in the second, Jesus appears to an individual, and the recognition scene leads on to a larger audience. In Jn. 20:1-18 three basic narratives are combined. The first, vv. 1-2, ii-13, shows the visit of women followers of Jesus to the tomb. We have here the earliest form of an empty tomb narrative found in any gospel. However, true to form, John has reduced the original group of women to Mary Magdalene for his own dramatic purposes, preparing the way for the later christophany to her. It is this christophany, and not an angelic spokesman, which explains the meaning of the empty tomb. Thus, John also changed the purpose for which the angels were introduced.

The Beloved Disciple.

In vv. 3-10, disciples, notably Peter, visit the tomb on hearing the women's report; this is the second narrative in the scene. The disciples find the tomb empty, then go away perplexed. Originally, Peter was, in the tradition, accompanied by an unnamed disciple. John has introduced this other as the beloved disciple, the 'disciple whom Jesus loved', so that his coming to faith might interpret the significance of the empty tomb. In 20:8 the phrase, 'he saw and believed' refers only to the Beloved Disciple: he is the ideal disciple whom all others should follow, he is *the* Christian. John's lesson is that love for Jesus gives the insight to perceive his presence. This disciple outdistances Peter because he loves Jesus more. Then, because he is closest to Jesus, he is also the first to look for him and to believe.

Mary Magdalene.

The third basic narrative in this scene is that of Jesus'

appearance to Mary Magdalene (20:14-18). Together with Mt. 28:9-10 and Mk. 16:9-11, this is the third independent form of a christophany to her. In the recognition scene, John wishes to teach that the risen Jesus has undergone a change from the Jesus of the ministry. Mary clings to Jesus because she is holding the source of all her joy. In telling her not to lay hold of him, Jesus is saying that his permanent presence is not to be by his fleshly appearance but by the gift of the Spirit. This can come only when he has ascended. So, instead of holding on to him, Mary is bidden to go and prepare the disciples for that coming of Jesus when the Spirit will be given.

Ascension.

The Risen Jesus is not restored to natural life, but to eternal life in God's presence. 'Ascension' is no more than a spatial term to describe his ineffable glorification and exaltation. In fact, the traditional 'resurrection' does not easily fit into John's theology of the crucifixion. Yet, John had to accommodate the tradition by trying to fit the resurrection into his view of the process whereby Jesus passed to his Father. For him there is a single hour: Jesus is lifted up on the cross, raised from the dead, and goes to the Father. The appearance to Mary Magdalene is a vehicle of his re-interpreted dramatization of the resurrection. It must be remembered that John is here trying to fit his theology of the resurrection/ascension, which has no dimension of time and space, into a narrative which must necessary be sequential. When Jesus says he is 'about to ascend' he is not referring to a time lag, but is identifying the resurrection with the ascension. It is meaningful for us that Mary knows Jesus only after he has called her by name. It is just as he had said in speaking of himself as the Good Shepherd: 'the sheep hear his voice, and he calls his own sheep by name and leads them out' (10:3).

The Spirit.

In the final scene of John's resurrection narrative

(20:19-29), Jesus appears to the disciples, showing them his hands and his side and bestowing on them the peace he had promised them in the Farewell Discourse. As in the Synoptics, John then shows Jesus entrusting a salvific mission to those to whom he has appeared. Their mission is closely related to his breathing new life upon them through his Spirit. The task of the Spirit is to take Jesus' place by carrying on his work and being his presence in the world. He also gives the disciples power over sin: men are to be divided (by their own self-judgment) into two groups — those who receive Jesus and those who do not recognize him. The most significant episode is that of Thomas' profession of faith. He provides the final example in the chapter of different attitudes of faith in the Risen Jesus. Thomas' cry, 'My Lord and my God! ' is the supreme christological statement of John's gospel. It is a liturgical confession, a response of praise to the God who has revealed himself in Jesus. And, of course, it leads to Jesus' blessing upon those who believe without having seen. When Jesus lived among men, faith had to be found through the visible and tangible. Now the era of signs and appearances is passing away, for the Spirit, or invisible presence of Jesus, shall make possible another realm of believing.

Faith.

In John's message what is important is to BELIEVE, whether that faith comes through seeing or not. In this beatitude ('Blessed are those who have not seen and yet believe') Jesus is contrasting two types of blessedness: they are the two different situations in which his disciples could find themselves. He is assuring all readers of his gospel, all Christians, that those who are coming later and who will not see Jesus are equal, in God's eyes, to those who lived with him, saw him and thus were, in a certain sense, privileged. 'Blessed are those who have not seen and yet believe! ' The words bear the mark of the timeless Word spoken before the world was made. Whereas, in the synoptics, the risen Jesus takes leave of his disciples, the Johannine Jesus is not said to have departed. Through the Paraclete Spirit he remains present to his disciples to be with them forever, as comforting as his former presence in their midst (14:16f).

The Road to Emmaus.

In his delightful narrative of the Risen Lord and the two disciples on the road to Emmaus (24:13-35), Luke has, in his own way, taken the resurrection out of the past and brought it into our present. On Easter Day, Clopas and a companion, both disciples of Jesus, set out in sadness from Jerusalem, now the grave of their hopes, for the village of Emmaus. As they discussed the shattering experience of the preceding days. Jesus appeared, evidently as though he had overtaken them. The two do not at first recognize the Lord; as in similar appearances, a word or sign from him is needful before he is recognized. Jesus is going to prepare them for his self-revelation. At his question, 'What is this conversation which you are holding with each other as you walk? ', they stopped short, saddened by the import of it and amazed that one coming from Jerusalem could be ignorant of what had taken place. The disciples acknowledge that Jesus was a mighty prophet; but they had seen in him something more – the Messiah. Their disillusionment is forcefully expressed: before the death of Jesus they could still hope for a divine intervention – which might have taken place immediately after death, but certainly not as late as the third day! The situation had been aggravated by the report of some women; momentary hopes were dashed when disciples, investigating the matter, had found only an empty tomb. For the two Jesus is dead and with him their faith in him. They had not accepted all that the prophets had spoken. They had closed their eyes to the suffering of the Messiah; that is why the death of Jesus had been a fatal stumbling block. But, in God's design, the way to glory was the path of suffering: 'Was it not

necessary that the Christ should suffer these things and
enter into his glory?' Jesus explained to them the messianic prophecies — a precious testimony to a christian
interpretation of the Old Testament. It is noteworthy that
his exposition echoes the theme, and the very words, of
the *kerygma*, the mission preaching, of the early Church,
as we find it in the discourses of the first part of Acts:
apostolic testimony and the Scriptures bear witness to
Jesus of Nazareth who died and rose again.

The Breaking of Bread.

The breaking of bread is the occasion of the disciples'
recognition of the Lord. The expression 'breaking of
bread' is a technical term for the Eucharist and, in describing this meal, Luke has deliberately used eucharistic
language: Jesus took bread, blessed and broke it, gave it
to them. And his lesson is that as the two disciples recognized Jesus in the setting of a meal shared with him, so
Christians, in the eucharistic meal, make the same real
encounter with their Lord. Their eyes had been opened.
But Jesus had vanished from their sight, for now they
believed that he was truly risen. This whole passage,
centred around the 'liturgy of the word' (vv. 19-27) and
the 'eucharistic meal' (vv. 30f) has a liturgical coloring. It
is an early catechesis, in a liturgical setting, highlighting
the meeting with the Risen Lord in the Eucharist. It
brings home to us the truth of Jesus' beatitude: 'Blessed
are those who have not seen and yet believe' (Jn. 20:29).

"Then he led them out near Bethany,
  and with hands upraised, blessed them.
As he blessed, he left them, and was taken up to
  heaven" (Lk. 24:50).

THE ASCENSION.

> *'Christ Jesus. . . who is at the right hand of God'.*

The fact of Easter has been expressed in terms of resurrection; it is also in the New Testament expressed in terms of exaltation. Jesus was not only 'raised from the dead', he was also 'lifted up', 'exalted', he 'ascended' to heaven. It is not possible to be precise about the relationship of resurrection and exaltation. These may have been, originally, independent interpretations of the same event. Or it may be that the exaltation theme gives the resurrection of Jesus its full meaning. It makes clear, for instance, that the resurrection of Jesus was no return to earthly life, but a passage to new iife. What is sure is that the terms do not stand for two events but for two aspects of a single mystery. Of course there was a tendency, as an attempt to bring out the significance of the Christ-event, to set these aspects in chronological order. The sermon of Peter in Acts 2:2-36 is a case in point, with its sequence of death (v. 23), resurrection (vv. 24-32), ascension (v. 33), and enthronement (vv. 34-36). John has expressed a similar concern in his 'glorification' theology. The incarnate Son of Man who had come from the Father in the first place, ascends, returns to the Father, by way of being 'lifted up' on the cross. His exaltation on the cross was the beginning of a movement that culminated in resurrection and ascension. It is a profound theological interpretation of the cross, justified by christian faith in the risen Lord.

Ascension.

In Acts 1:9-11 Luke describes an ascension of the risen Christ. He is the only New Testament writer to do so, and he has closed his gospel, too, with a briefer description of the ascension (Lk. 24:50-53). In the latter passage he has undoubtedly given the impression that all the events of ch. 24, including the ascension, had taken place on Easter Sunday. Matthew would seem to agree that all had indeed happened on Easter Day. While he does not speak of an ascension, he lets it be understood, by the declaration of Jesus on the fulness of power which was now his (Mt. 28:18), that he had come to this meeting in Galilee from his heavenly throne. John, of course, is specific. At the meeting with Mary Magdalene Jesus tells her that he is going to his Father without delay, and he sends Mary to tell his brethren so (20:17).

Yet, in John, we have a brief delay between resurrection and ascension. This serves a pedagogical purpose: Jesus teaches Mary that he is not only risen, but has entered into a new state. The simple truth is that we do not know when the resurrection took place; but the resurrection certainly means that Jesus was *at once* with his Father. Our problem is not only the spatial one of earth and heaven but also the temporal one of time and eternity. Jesus, at his death, entered into, passed over into, his new life. But his disciples, and we through them, needed to be convinced of his victory over death and of his new life of glory. That is why we have the withdrawal of his earthly body and its transformation, why we have his showing himself to his disciples, and why we have Luke's description of his ascension.

We might safely assume that Luke does not wish to contradict himself and does not do so. While he asserts that Jesus appeared to the disciples 'during forty days' (Acts 1:3), he later speaks of an ascension after 'many days' (13:31), or omits any temporal indication (10:41). He is not, in fact, making an issue of 'forty days' as an exact period of time. This reference to forty is designed to link Easter and Pentecost; Luke wants to emphasize that the risen Christ sends the Holy Spirit. For, if Jesus returns definitively to heaven it is in order to give the Spirit who will henceforth take his place among the disciples.

Farewell.

The Ascension after a period of 'forty days' is the final leave-taking of Christ; now he will no longer come from the presence of the Father to appear to the disciples as he did during the short time after the resurrection. It should be clear that the liturgical feast of Ascension Day commemorating his final departure is not in conflict with the other tradition of the one movement of resurrection-ascension. In the course of time, however, emphasis fell altogether on the final ascension and the other aspect of the mystery was lost to sight. We had, for long, seemingly uncritically accepted the apparent delay between resurrection and ascension. We had failed to ask the obvious question, Why? – or the even more obvious one, Where was Jesus during those forty days?

When we compare the various New Testament texts we discover, in the mystery of the elevation of Christ, two connected but distinct aspects: on the one hand the heavenly glorification of Jesus which coincided with his resurrection; on the other hand his final departure after a period of appearances, a departure and return to God witnessed by a group of disciples on the Mount of Olives and celebrated in the liturgical feast of the Ascension. But what took place on that occasion? The only description of the event, Acts 1:9-11, is cast in the stereotyped language of theophany. In this language, 'cloud' veils (and at the same time reveals the presence of) the divine, or is the vehicle of divinity. In Acts the phrase, 'and a cloud took him out of their sight', has both aspects: the risen

Lord is borne away into the heavenly sphere. The 'two men' are the angel spokesmen who explain the meaning of the episode. The witnesses had indeed, in what manner we cannot say, experienced the departure of their Lord, and they knew, with conviction, that this was the end of that first, privileged moment. Now the Risen One had withdrawn, until the end of time, his visible presence from the world. His visible presence — for he does not abandon them, does not leave them orphans. Moreover, 'he will come in the same way as you saw him go up into heaven'. Christ, victor over death, has opened up a new world of life with God. He has entered first, to prepare a place for his elect, then he will return to take them with him that they may be with him always (Jn. 14:2-3).

Joy.

Christ had left the world and returned to the Father. Yet, it is not incongruous that in his gospel mention of the ascension, Luke states that after the Lord had parted from them the disciples 'returned to Jerusalem *with great joy*' (24:52). This surprising joy is explained not only by their realization that 'the Lord has risen indeed' (v. 34), nor only by the assurance that, very soon, they will be 'clothed with power from on high' (v. 49). There is, besides, the conviction that the Lord, whom they had seen depart, had not really left them at all. This conviction of the abiding presence of the Lord is so evident in Paul. But it is present, too, in a particularly touching way, in Revelation 2-3 — the letters to the Seven Churches. Christ is no absentee landlord, administering his Church through an agent or agents: he himself is present in and to the Christian communities.

Mission.

In the apparition stories of the Risen Lord we find, prevalently, a pattern of initiative, recognition, and mission. The Lord appears and shows himself to the disciples. They do not realize that it is he until some familiar word ('Mary! ') or gesture ('they knew him in the breaking of bread') leads to their recognition of him. He has a task for them: 'As the Father has sent me, even so I send you' (Jn. 20-21). The One with the Father forever is still present in his Church, is still active in the world in and through the men and women of his calling. We can find inspiration and comport in two gospel accounts of the final testament of the Lord.

Last Instruction (Lk. 24:44-49).

At the close of his gospel Luke summarizes the last commission of Jesus to his disciples — repeated at the beginning of Acts (1:3-8). Jesus recalls the occasions on which he had warned the disciples that he, in fulfillment of the will of God enshrined in Scripture, would have to suffer and die, and rise again. Then he gives them a new understanding of the Old Testament, an insight that will enable them to see how and where it 'bears witness to him'. This reinterpretation of the Old Testament is a basic element of the primitive kerygma which proclaimed the dawning of the age of fulfillment involving the suffering of the Messiah and his resurrection on the third day. The kerygma, as here, always includes the proclamation of repentance and forgiveness of sin, a proclamation to all men. This message of salvation will go forth from Jerusalem, preached by the apostles who are witnesses of the fulfillment of the promise, men who have seen the risen Christ and who can attest that this Lord is the same Jesus with whom they had lived. The disciples are convincing witnesses and efficacious missionaries because they have seen the Lord and have believed in him; all who would, effectively, bear witness to Christ must have encountered him in personal and living faith. Today, when the call of the apostolate is urgent and the role of witness is seen as the obligation of every Christian, we are more keenly aware that religion is not the acknowledgment of a body of doctrine or the adherence to a code of laws, but attachment to a Person. Knowledge of Christ, knowledge in the biblical sense of acceptance and commitment, is the

essence of christian life; it is evidently the first require-
ment of an apostle. The Good News is the proclamation
of events that manifestly followed a pattern traced by
God, the fulfillment of a divine purpose. It was inevitable
that this proclamation, in part couched in terms of the
Old Testament, should itself become a new chapter in the
written word of God.

The Great Commission (Mt. 28:18-20)

This text, the final word in his gospel, has been seen
to recapitulate the whole of Matthew. It is also one of
the most comforting assurances which the Christian could
hear that the risen Jesus lives on among us. Although
Jesus speaks as the *Kyrios* here, the kernel of his message
is not his own person but the missionary command. He
speaks the language of Matthew and of the Lord living in
Matthew's community. The sayings had not been spoken
by Jesus on earth, but have been wrought by the apostolic Church. They are however (like the Johannine
discourses) authentic expressions of his mind – and so are
the words of the Lord on earth.

Power.

Jesus' saying that 'all power has been given to me' is
directly influenced by Dan. 7:14, where we read that
power was granted to the Son of man. But in Daniel it is
a matter of earthly power over humans, whereas in Matthew is is divine power in heaven and on earth. The
command, 'Go, therefore, and make disciples of all nations' implies that God no longer limits his saving grace to
Israel but turns his mercy to the Gentiles. Salvation will
come to the nations through their union in Jesus. While
in Daniel the nations are ordained to serve the Son of
man, here they will be invited to become disciples of
Jesus. It is not a process of subjection but of being drawn
to Jesus through persuasion and grace. 'Teaching them all
that I have commanded you': the baptized, the one
taught or the 'disciple', is he who observes Jesus' com-

mands. 'All' his commands consists of the true life of God's people, as in Deuteronomy.

Promise.

Finally, we have Jesus' great promise of v. 20: 'Lo, I am with you always, to the close of the age'. Here, in his very last words, Matthew opens out into the perspective of the Community. It corresponds to the 'hereafter' of 26:64, where Jesus told Caiaphas, 'hereafter you will see the Son of man seated at the right hand of Power...' Jesus is promising his help, as God himself, echoing all his assurances throughout the gospels: 'Fear not! '; 'I am with you! ', 'It is I! '. Whereas Luke closes with a farewell blessing and the ascension (Lk. 24:51), here in Matthew Jesus assures us that he will be abidingly present in the congregation. Moreover, what is present is not his static presence in one chosen group, but his dynamic and helping presence for a worldwide mission. It is the mission of salvation: the name *Immanu-el*, 'God-with-us' is perfectly realized in the name and work of *Jesus*, 'God saves'.

Matthews finale both assigns to Jesus the function of Yahweh in the Old Testament and sums up Matthew's view of the *Kyrios* in the New. He has universal lordship; he gives commands that determine the whole life of God's people and their relationship to him; and he promises to be the sustaining Lord at all times. Will he not keep his word? 'Where two or three are gathered in my name, there am I in the midst of them' (Mt. 18:20).

"You will receive power when the Holy Spirit comes down on you; then you are to be my witnesses in Jerusalem, throughout Judea and Samaria, yes, even to the ends of the earth" (Acts 1:8).

THE DESCENT OF THE HOLY SPIRIT.

'Receive the Holy Spirit'.

'I will not leave you desolate. I will come to you' (Jn. 14:18). If the risen Lord had visibly withdrawn from the sight and touch of his followers, he had by no means abandoned them. His word to Mary Magdalene – 'Do not hold me' – is meant to teach her, and us, that circumstances and his condition have changed. He is no longer the familiar friend of the past, but he is no less Friend. His presence now, among his own, will not be in the figure of the Man of Galilee, but as the life-giving Spirit.

Pentecost.

The Lucan account of Pentecost describes the beginning of the new era of the Church. Luke has rightly seen that this new thing could come to birth only through the Spirit of God. Following on the third gospel which, more than the other synoptics, underlines the action of the Holy Spirit in the ministry of Jesus, Acts gives the impression that the first christian community lived entirely under the movement of the Spirit; Acts is like a 'gospel of the Spirit'. Before his ascension, his farewell, the Risen Christ had assured his disciples that he would send upon them the promised gift of the messianic age, the Holy Spirit, who would empower them to carry out their task of witnesses to Jesus (Lk. 24:47-49; Acts 1:5,8). The fulfillment of the promise was the baptism of the Spirit'

(Acts 1:5) of Pentecost. This marked the beginning of the time of the Church just as the baptism in the Jordan inaugurated the public ministry of the Savior; in both cases Luke insists on the sensible manifestation of the Spirit (Lk. 3:22; Acts 2:3).

Here too, as in their communication with the Risen Lord, we are dealing with a wholly real, but essentially spiritual and interior, experience of the disciples. The historical basis of Luke's Pentecost narrative would appear to be the first public proclamation of Christ. His solemn introduction to the episode — 'When the day of Pentecost was fulfilled' — indicates that the disciples had waited for this moment. In Old Testament thought, the Spirit of God is not only a mighty wind but a consuming fire; Luke has combined these images. Under this powerful influence, the disciple's spoke in tongues', in ecstatic prayer. Luke has chosen to regard the phenomenon as a speaking in 'other tongues', thus dramatically presenting the real significance of the outpouring of the Spirit: this preaching of the Good News, in their own languages, to representatives of the known world, is the inauguration of a worldwide mission. In his subsequent discourse, Peter explained that the ecstatic speaking in tongues was a sign that the Risen Christ had indeed poured out his Spirit upon them (Acts 2:33), thus fulfilling the prophecy of Joel. Since, however, Joel had spoken of 'all flesh', the gift of the Holy Spirit is not for the circle of disciples alone but for all who believe in Christ. Peter, then, can assure his hearers that they too will receive the Spirit if they will believe and be baptized (2:38f) — not only they but 'all that are far off, every one whom the Lord our God calls to him' (2:39). Possession of the Spirit is part of the equipment of the Christian.

The Spirit in the Church.

While the presence of the Spirit is manifest in charisms (10:46; 19:6) and prophecy (11:28; 21:11f; 13:1; 15:32; 21:9) his role as guide and sustainer of the christian preachers is of far greater importance. In the strength of the Spirit just received Peter bore witness before the crowd of Jews and proselytes (2:5f) to Jesus as the Messiah sent by God (2:22-36). The witness of the apostles is specifically designated the work of the Spirit (5:32). His enemies cannot withstand a Stephen filled with 'wisdom and the Spirit' (6:10). The Spirit directs the apostles and leaders of the community and dictates their line of conduct: 'the Spirit said to Philip' (8:29); 'the Spirit said to Peter' (10:19). Peter was enlightened by the Spirit in the crucial matter of the acceptance of the Gentile Cornelius into the christian community (10:19; 11:12); and when the whole question of Gentile converts was in the balance, the Spirit guided the apostolic council (15:28). The Spirit called Barnabas and Saul to the first Gentile mission and directed the church at Antioch to set them apart for that task (13:2-4). In short, the Spirit is the principal mover in the decisive events of Acts. In this way Luke demonstrates that the gift of the Spirit did indeed mark the inauguration of the era of church and mission, the new age of salvation history.

The Paraclete.

On the evening of Easter Sunday — in John's chronology — Jesus came from the presence of his Father and manifested himself to his disciples. It is because he was now fully 'glorified', by his death, resurrection, and exaltation, that he can give them the gift of the Spirit (Jn. 20:22), for the Spirit was not given until then (7:39). John's description of the death of Jesus is in line with this: 'and bowing his head, he handed over the spirit' (19:30). Now already glorified on the cross, he handed over the Holy Spirit — specifically to his Mother who, at that solemn moment stood for the new people of God, the Church, and to the Beloved Disciple, who symbolized the Christian. In John, too, the gift of the Spirit is closely related to the sending of the disciples as missionaries into the world (20:21-22). In this respect, the situation is quite like the Pentecost setting of Acts. But John and Luke approach the matter differently, and we cannot assume that one speaks of an earlier giving of the Spirit and the other of a second, later giving. Each in his own way is describing the same event: the one gift of the Spirit to his followers by the risen and exalted Lord. The dating of the event differs widely but the arrangement, in each case, reflects the diverse theological interests of the evangelists. The central facts are that both evangelists place the giving of the Spirit after Jesus had ascended to the Father and that, for both, the Spirit's role is to take the place of Jesus, to carry on his work and to constitute his presence in the world.

In John, most clearly, the Spirit is presented as the divine power that continues and completes Jesus' ministry; the Spirit is the perpetuation of Jesus' presence among his followers. The Spirit is the principle of the divine sonship that Jesus has made possible for men; John's emphasis is on the Spirit as sanctifier and as source of the life of the Christian. The activity of the Paraclete (his designation of the Spirit) is to reveal the mind of Christ, to bring out the implication of his person and his message. We live not by the words of the "historical" Jesus but by the words of the Lord made known through the Church enlightened by the Spirit.

This becomes more understandable, indeed obvious, if we accept that, for John, the paraclete is 'the personal presence of Jesus in the Christian while Jesus is with the Father' (R. E. Brown). The one whom Jesus calls 'another Paraclete' is another Jesus. 'As yet the Spirit had not been given, because Jesus was not yet glorified' (7:39) — if, then, the Spirit can only come when Jesus departs, the Spirit/Paraclete is the presence of the 'absent' Jesus. As Paraclete, the glorified Lord is abidingly present in his Church. In this way, the later Christian is assured that he is no further removed from the time of the ministry of Jesus than the earlier Christian, for the Paraclete dwells within him as fully as Jesus 'abode' in his disciples.

The Spirit of God.

For Paul the Spirit is primarily the Spirit of God. But he is, too, the Spirit of Christ — indeed, Christ is 'a life-giving Spirit' (1 Cor. 15:45). We may well find this fluctuation surprising, as, no doubt, we find surprising John's understanding of the Paraclete. It is less surprising when we realize that what we have in the New Testament is the basis of our later theology of the Trinity, and not that trinitarian theology. Besides, the Spirit of God cannot be separated from the Father and the Son; he is revealed with them in Jesus Christ. We need to remember that God is One. The Spirit reminds us, pressingly, that God is Mystery, and prevents us from forgetting that 'God is Spirit' (Jn. 4:24) and that 'the Lord is the Spirit' (1 Cor. 3:17). Christ, the Revealer of the Godhead, is the Revealer of the Spirit. And, through Christ, the Spirit of God is present in the Christian. For Paul it is enough that through the Christ-event the Spirit of God is present and at work in the world and in men. He does not find it necessary to specify the relationship of the Spirit to Christ and to the Father.

The Spirit of Christ.

In Paul, the Spirit is basically a divine and heavenly dynamic force which exists in a special way in the risen Christ and pervades his Body, the Church. Paul is interested in the functional role of this Spirit in man's salvation. The 'Spirit of Christ' is both the gift of God's presence to men and the way in which new life is communicated to men. Paul can say, too, that it is the Holy Spirit who, together with Christ, brings about this renewal, this new birth: 'You were washed, you were sanctified, you were justified, in the name of our Lord Jesus Christ and in the Spirit of our God' (1 Cor. 6:11). The Spirit makes the Christian aware that he is, in a real sense, a child of God. He gives him the true attitude of a child of God, an attitude of love and confidence. It is thanks to the Holy Spirit that the Christian can dare to address God as 'Father'.

> For all who are led by the Spirit of God are sons of God. For you did not receive the spirit of slavery to fall back into fear, but you have received the spirit of sonship. When we cry, 'Abba! Father! ' it is the Spirit himself bearing witness with our spirit that we are children of God (Rom. 8:14-16).

The Holy Spirit speaks to the heart of God's child and convinces him that he really is a child of God. And the Spirit inspires him to call God by the same familiar name that Jesus used: *Abba*. In doing so, the Spirit 'speaks what he hears' and 'takes what is of Jesus' and declares it (Jn. 16:13,15); for, it is the Son who makes us sons. The Christian, in being taught how to address his Father, learns of the confidence he should have in him. But we must act like children of a loving Father – we must be moved by love. We ought not be forced to act by laws and commandments; we should be inspired, moved interiorly, by the Spirit of love. And the Holy Spirit can move us from within, because he dwells in us. If, then, the Spirit does dwell in us, our whole conduct should be inspired by him: 'If we live by the Spirit, let us also walk by the Spirit' (Gal. 5:25).

The Spirit is opposed to all that Paul calls the 'flesh': unregenerate human nature, man as the subject of sin. Christian life is a constant tension, a constant struggle between the demands of the 'flesh' and the will of God, between the slavery of sin and filial love of God. Gradually, the Spirit transforms the sinner into a true child of God, the slave into a free man, the broken, defeated man into a conqueror. And last, at the end of all, he will lead the faithful Christian to the glory of the resurrection: 'If the Spirit of him who raised Jesus from the dead dwells in you, he who raised Christ Jesus from the dead will give life to your mortal bodies also, through his Spirit which dwells in you' (Rom. 8:11).

Holiness.

The 'law' of the Spirit is, in the first place a *rule of holiness*. This means that we are to belong to God, that we are consecrated to him. By the fact that the Christian is subject to the action of the Holy Spirit he is opposed to the 'world' — fallen mankind, alienated from God and hostile to Christ — and gradually purified from sin. By that very fact he belongs to God and is consecrated to him. He is 'holy' or 'sacred' in that sense. This is brought out more decisively in another passage: 'Do you not know that you are God's temple and that God's Spirit dwells in you? ... For God's temple is holy, and that temple you are' (1 Cor. 3:16f). Thanks, then, to the Holy Spirit who dwells within us, we are temples of God, we are consecrated to God's service. We should strive to live accordingly. And we should be continually grateful to God who has chosen us 'from the beginning to be saved through sanctification by the Spirit and belief in the truth' (2 Thes. 2:13).

Freedom.

The Spirit's guidance is a *law of liberty*. Paul saw, clearly, that without Christ man was in slavery — in the slavery of sin and death. Christ brought freedom, and the Spirit that he gave was the Spirit of liberty. And the law of the Spirit — his guiding hand — is not a burden which hampers men; it is a 'law' that sets men free: 'The law of the Spirit of life in Christ Jesus has set me free from the law of sin and death' (Rom. 8:2). Paul, former Pharisee that he was, believed passionately in freedom. He had known, too long, the slavery of a rigid religious system, the bondage of a religion of law and precept. Christ had set him free from all that — 'For freedom Christ has set us free! ' (Gal. 5:1) — and he gloried in his freedom. He ached for his disciples to value the freedom that was theirs; he was sad and angry when freedom was not truly appreciated: 'stand fast, therefore, and do not submit again to a yoke of slavery' (5:1). He understood, very

well, the awesome responsibility of freedom and scrupu-
lously respected the conscience of his disciples: he would
not compel them – they must make a personal decision.
But christian freedom is never licence to do as one
pleases; it is always motivated – and constrained – by
love. 'For though I am free from all men, I have made
myself a slave to all. . .' (1 Cor. 9:19). Paul found his
freedom in the Spirit. The 'law' of the Spirit is not
imposed on us, something outside ourselves; we are
moved interiorly, and we are moved freely. How free we
are we know only too well from our own experience, for
we can, and we do, turn a deaf ear to the promptings of
the Spirit. Unhappily, too, the gentle action of the Spirit
can be stifled in other ways. We have not had, nor do we
have as a rule, Paul's passion for christian freedom.

Love.

The law of the Spirit is a law of freedom precisely
because it is a *law of love*: 'God's love has been poured
into our hearts through the Holy Spirit which has been
given to us' (Rom. 5:5). For charity is the fulness and the
fulfilling of that one law which the law of the Spirit ultimately is. This is because love discerns *the* moment
whereas authority often seeks to make one formula of
words be always applicable at every moment. Paul has left
no room for doubt as to the importance and the absolute
necessity for love in the christian life. Throughout his
writings *agapē* can refer to the love of God and of Christ
for man, the love of man for God and Christ, and the
mutual love of Christians. When the word occurs by itself
it is sometimes impossible to determine whether it refers
directly to the love of God or to the love of Christians
for one another; but this situation flows from the very
nature of *agapē*. At any rate, Paul leaves us in no doubt
as to the importance of fraternal charity: 'For the whole
law is fulfilled in one word, "You shall love your neigh-
bor as yourself" '(Gal. 5:14; cf Rom. 13:9f). It is the

Spirit who enables us to love God and to love one another.

The Spirit makes us *holy* — consecrated to God and invulnerable to all that might defile us. He sets us *free* for he moves us from within and in listening to and following his gentle promptings we are supremely free. He is the Spirit of *love* — who fills us with love for God and moves us to express this love in love for our fellow men. He is all of that, if we do not turn a deaf ear to his promptings, if we do not put obstacles in his way. Paul has given the salutary warning not to 'grieve the Holy Spirit of God' (Eph. 4:30).

"*If we have been united to him in a death like his,
we shall certainly be united to him
in a resurrection like his ... We know that Christ being
raised from the dead will never die again*" (Rom.
6:3-11).

THE ASSUMPTION OF MARY.

'We know that we have passed out of death into life'.

At this point we leave, or apparently leave, the field of the Scriptures, and turn to that of dogma. The Assumption of Mary is not an assertion of Scripture but has been solemnly defined by the Church as a revealed truth. Yet, when we take the Assumption in a wider context, or call it by another name, we find that it has, after all, a firm scriptural basis. For, when all is said and done, what is the assumption of Mary but her *resurrection*? And the resurrection of the Christian is central to the faith and hope of Christians.

Assumption.

The dogmatic declaration of her assumption does indeed assert that Mary 'was assumed body and soul into heavenly glory'. The text implies that Mary had died. We would not be wide of the mark if we were to think that customarily the fact would be visualized rather like this: At death, Mary's soul was separated from her body. Then, with her soul restored to her now risen and transformed body, she was taken into the presence of God, to join the risen Christ in his glory. This view is hardly the biblical one. The neat soul/body dichotomy, so familiar to us, is not Scripture's view of man, nor is it, increasingly, a concept congenial to modern man. If we take death as, literally, a separation of soul and body, then we must be prepared to accept that *part* of man only survives death, and that at some point in the future, with the restoration of his body, man is whole again. Is this view realistic or acceptable? We seem, through our over-literal reading of Scripture, and the limitation of our time-bound horizon, to have painted ourselves into a corner.

Resurrection.

When we look to the firm New Testament assertion of the 'resurrection of the body', we find that the essence of it is an assertion of the reality of life beyond death. The manner of resurrection and the nature of the risen body are left vague, or, more often, not considered at all. Paul's intense desire 'to be dissolved and be with Christ' would hardly be achieved in a partial Pauline presence with Christ. The fact is that, for a Jew (and surely for us too) real life can only be, and must be, the life of a person; human life, even beyond death, must be 'bodily' life. The 'body' is not the structure of flesh and blood as such. The body which now partakes of the perishable substance of 'flesh' remains the same 'body' when, beyond death, it will partake of the imperishable substance of 'glory'. This involves a total transformation of the body, now become spiritual, incorruptible, and immortal (1 Cor. 15:35-53).

Life with Christ.

It seems that we should regard death as a transition. Human life is lived in two phases. There is the earth-bound, time-bound phase that we know so well. Then, at death, we pass over into the second and final phase, no longer circumscribed by earth and time. It is the life beyond death of our hope, a phase of life not yet of our experience before death. For the Christian it is life with Christ. The life after death is not a wholly new life: it is the life he has been living all the time in Christ, only lived under different conditions. When bodily death comes it is a matter of being 'away from the body and at home with the Lord' (cf 2 Cor. 5:6).

The dogma of the Assumption of Mary is the solemn assertion that one of our race, that she who is the type of the whole christian people does indeed live, here and now, the eternal life with Christ. 'She, who by faith has received salvation for herself and for us all, has received it *totally*, for it is the salvation of a *whole* human being' (K. Rahner). In her, we can already see our destiny. In her glorious resurrection we have the assurance that our christian death is a going to the Lord, to be with the Lord forever. But the believer already has eternal life; christian life, already, is anticipated resurrection-life. In this context of the risen glory of Mary we may profitably reflect on the significance of the Risen Lord for us here and now, the manifestation in us of the new life that he gives.

Death.

'Unless a grain of wheat falls into the earth and dies, it remains alone; but if it dies, it bears much fruit' (Jn. 12:24). Jesus' parabolic reference to his own imminent death contains the kernel of Christianity and its paradox. The road to Life leads through death; the meaning of living is grasped in dying. The christian attitude towards death should be to see it not as something negative but as something positive, something capable of bringing forth 'much fruit'. Of course, the fact of bodily death terminating life remains the decisive moment. Yet, the Christian must see death not so much as a boundary in a terminal sense, as a new horizon. Indeed, he must view it as an open door to the fulness of Life for which his entire earthly existence has been searching. Yet, it is not death in itself which gives a whole, unified existence to the Christian; rather it is resurrection. Just as John saw Jesus' death, resurrection, and exaltation to glory as a single moment, so too, the Christian is to see the life to come as a continuation of the process of dying.

Life.

Paul taught that to be a follower of Jesus means in one sense to have already died: to be baptized into Jesus meant also to be baptized into his death, and to be united to his resurrection-life (Rom. 6:3-8). The Christian had died, and his life is 'hid with Christ in God' (Col. 5:3). And so (could we but believe!) the moment of death is for us the moment of true life — simply because it is the moment of perfect communion, fellowship, with Jesus and his Father. It is Jesus who has made this possible for us.

The resurrection of Jesus does not mean only that he has overcome death for us by giving us a vague hope of rising with him one day. Far more it means that he has overcome all that would keep us from living fully each day. It means that he gives a new, deeper dimension to *life*: 'I have come that you may have life, and have it more abundantly' — to the full (Jn. 10:10). He has come that we may rise with him each new dawn breaking over the skies. 'Because I live', he says, 'you too shall live' (14:19).

Could we find any meaning to life here on earth did we not have the Hope that life on this earth is not the end of all? All that we suffer and strive for, all that we cannot understand, even all our real (but momentary) joys — do these not fall into their proper perspective when we see them in the Hope-light of the resurrection, of a life above and beyond them all? Christians live life because they have the hope of the resurrection. The resurrection-life is what Jesus calls 'real life, 'life indeed', 'eternal life'. It is so important to try to grasp this — to grasp that this 'eternal life' is not a temporal concept denoting life after death, something quantitative. Rather, it is qualitative: it denotes a different condition of life made possible by the coming of Jesus.

Crucifixion.

But we may never forget that the resurrection of Jesus

came to pass only through the crucifixion! In Jesus, the everlasting pattern in the nature of things, this pattern that life comes only through death, reaches its peak. It becomes personalized in the most perfect way: it is God himself who must die to rise. It is the great paschal mystery of Christendom. Christ our passover lamb is sacrificed. Let us therefore *celebrate. . .!*

This is a leading thought of John: Jesus' crucifixion, resurrection, and glorification constitute a single moment, the one 'hour' of Jesus' whole accomplishment of his Father's work for him. It is because he must 'go away' for a little while in death that he can come to us anew in life. It is also the leitmotif in all Paul's epistles: 'We preach Christ crucified, a stumbling block to Jews and folly to the Gentiles – but to us who are called, Christ the power of God and the wisdom of God' (1 Cor. 1:22-24). Through his own failure, sufferings, and personal feebleness, Paul understood the 'scandal' of the Cross which he felt compelled to preach. It is because he shared in the 'fellowship of Jesus' sufferings' that he was confident also of sharing in 'the power of his resurrection' (Phil. 3:10). He was aware of having been crucified to himself so that only Christ lived in him (Gal. 2:20). He had absolute confidence:

> If we have been united to him in a death like his, we shall certainly be united to him in a resurrection like his. . . We know that Christ being raised from the dead will never die again. Death no longer has dominion over him. . . So you must consider yourselves dead to sin and alive to God in Christ Jesus (Rom. 6:3-11).

The Present Lord.

Emphasis on the resurrection developed in one way from the situation of the early Church in which the Parousia and the final age were no longer counted as imminent. Christians began to concentrate on the great fact of Easter and what Jesus Christ had already provided for

them – the mustard seed he had already planted, the
leaven he had already set into the dough. But, in another
way, all that realized eschatology or the resurrection life
means can be said to have sprung from the experience of
people like ourselves. These were the men and women of
the early christian community who actually found that
Jesus was truly living on in the heart of each of them,
that he was present to them through the Holy Spirit
which he had sent according to his promise. They found:
'where two or three are gathered in my name, there am I
in the midst of them' (Mt. 18:20). Through baptism and
the eucharist and through worshipping together, the early
Christians came to realize that they were indeed sharing
in the life of Jesus. He and his Father had come to make
their home among them (Jn. 14:28).

In Christ.

Man makes himself open to the effects of the Christ-
event through the experience of faith, a vital personal
commitment. This experience is not something external to
man but affects his inmost being: it is an intimate union
with God in Christ. Somehow, the Christian exists and
lives as a Christian in virtue of the life that comes to him
from the risen Christ – God has brought it about that he
has life in Christ Jesus (1 Cor. 1:30); he is created anew
in Christ Jesus (2 Cor. 5:17). The prepositional phrase *en
Christō* ('in Christ'). which occurs frequently in Paul's
writings, points, – when taken in a vertical sense – to a
relationship with Christ in person, an incorporation that
becomes a symbiosis of Christ and the Christian. To live
in Christ, to exist in Christ, means that the life of a Christian is a life flowing from his union with Christ who is its
source and author by his living presence in the believer.

Christ in us.

This follows, perhaps more obviously, from another expression – the obverse of the other and its complement –
which occurs less frequently: Christ lives, is, in the Chris-

tian. Paul can say: 'it is no longer I who live, but Christ who lives in me' (Gal. 2:20). He can ask the Corinthians to remind themselves, to bring themselves to a fuller realization of the fact that Jesus Christ is in them (2 Cor. 13:5; cf Rom. 8:9-11; Eph. 3:17). Thus, if the Christian exists and lives in Christ so, too, Christ lives in the Christian. From different points of view both formulas express the same relationship, the union of Christ with believers. One is reminded of the Johannine *menein* ('to abide'). We hear in John that just as the Son is in the Father, and the Father is in the Son (14:10f), so the disciples are to abide in the Son as he abides in them (15:4-10). It would seem that the two great theologians, each in his own way, are struggling to put into inadequate human words the ultimately ineffable reality of union with Christ.

The Christian.

The Christian is altogether dependent on Christ – all comes from him. There cannot be a Christian except in terms of Christ; after all, that is what the name implies. Paul can declare that, in Christ, all differences go: all Christians form one in Christ: 'As many of you as were baptized into Christ have put on Christ. There is neither Jew nor Gentile, there is neither slave nor free, there is neither male nor female; for you are all one in Christ Jesus' (Gal. 3:27f). This text focuses our attention on the other dimension of the formula 'in Christ' – the horizontal dimension. The Christ-life in the Christian finds expression, incarnational expression, in christian living. One force alone can overcome the divisions inherent in humanity ('Jew and Gentile... slave and free'): the power of love. It is the hallmark of the life of Jesus and must mark the life of the Christian; it alone 'binds everything together into perfect harmony' (Col. 3:14). Love necessarily involves others; only in community can a life that is characterized by love be lived. A Christian cannot be autonomous nor live his life in isolation; others are essential to this mode of being. The Christian community enables the individual to be authentically human.

Heaven.

But, our life on earth still ends in death. For the Christian there is the firm hope of life beyond death; and the assumption of Mary is a promise of heaven. In a welter of speculation and imagination about heaven we have the one comforting assurance of its essentially christological structure, for this ensures the truly human aspect of it. 'Heaven is based on Jesus Christ's conquest of death and on his exaltation, which are the preconditions for the ability of creatures to enter the life of God himself; this abiding of personal creatures in the presence of God essentially means the gathering of mankind into the definitive Body of Christ, into the "whole Christ", to commune with God who is made (and remains) *man*; hence it is that we shall "see one another again", that the human relationships of this world continue in heaven. This union of man with God and with his fellows means no loss or absorption of individuality; rather the closer man approaches to God the more his individuality is liberated and fortified'. (K. Rahner).

"God who is mighty has done great things for me,
    holy is his name;
His mercy is from age to age
    on those who fear him" (Lk. 1: 49-50).

MARY, QUEEN OF HEAVEN.

> *'Henceforth all generations will call me blessed'.*

'Queen of Heaven' is a title that evokes, too readily, the florid litany of Loreto. It is more comforting to reflect that, if Mary is queen, it is in the sense in which Jesus is king: 'My kingship is not of this world' (Jn. 18:36). Mary is too important for Christianity to be the victim of questionable theology. Happily, we can now look to the final chapter of Vatican II's Dogmatic Constitution on the Church (*Lumen Gentium*) for an authentic statement of Mariology. That we can end our study of the theological basis of the Rosary in terms of a twentieth-century event underlines the freshness of this venerable prayer.

'The word 'compromise' is often suspect, but it can have a thoroughly reasonable significance. It can mean, not a watering-down, not the surrender of a principle, but a realistic bowing to truth as something greater than any human reflection of it. That the fathers of Vatican II did compromise, and ended up by treating of Mary not in isolation but in the context of their treatment of the Church, is not a triumph of Marian 'minimalists' over Marian 'maximalists'. It represents a sane and balanced appreciation of the place of Mary. It is somehow parallel to what we have noted of the sage perception of our Greek and Russian brethren: that Mary is not to be seen in isolation from her Son. Vatican II has emphasized that Mary is not to be seen in isolation from the Church of her Son.

The final chapter of *Lumen Gentium*, consecrated to Mary, is significantly entitled: 'The Blessed Virgin Mary, Mother of God, in the Mystery of Christ and the Church'. The question was how Mary's position, and the devotion of the faithful to her, could be better explained: as a figure apart, or in a context which should bring out her importance in the work of our redemption. In the event, we were treated to an aspect of what was, in general, a feature of Vatican II, the fact of one, particularist, theology yielding to the impact of a more representative theology. Here we shall merely point to the salient aspects of Vatican II's mariology.

Born of Woman.

The Preface to chapter 8 of *Lumen Gentium*, which presents the place of Mary in christian faith and theology, highlights the seemingly pale (mariologically speaking) text of Paul: 'When the time had fully come, God sent forth his Son. born of woman . . . so that we might receive adoption as sons' (Gal. 4:4f). Christologically, it is a rich text which asserts that Christ is true man because he was born of woman and true Son of God because God is his Father. Read against the infancy gospels of Matthew and Luke, it implies that Mary is in truth the Mother of God.

Mother of God.

Mother of God – Mary's status involves two principles, neither of which may be sacrificed to the other. As Mother of God, Mary is the privileged daughter of the Father and the temple of the Holy Spirit; as fully human, redeemed, she is a member of the Church (albeit a supereminent member who is the archetype of the Church. But always it is her relation to Christ, her link with him, that matters. Because Christ's work of redemption is abidingly present in the Church, it is needful to look too to the position which Mary holds in the Church, to see her place in his body and, consequently, the duties towards Mary that the redeemed have. She 'occupies a place in the Church which is the highest after Christ and also the closest to us' (art. 54).

With commendable caution, *Lumen Gentium* presents Mary's part in saving history. Notably, it states: 'she stands out among the poor and humble of the Lord' (art. 55). She is, more fully than Simeon or Anna, one of the *anawim*: this is why the Magnificat, a song of the *anawim*, is so fittingly her song. Yet she is, too, the Daughter of Zion: mother of the Messiah and of the messianic people. Mary's assent to the coming of the Savior, expressed in her own *Fiat*, was the assent of faith of the people which she represents. She, in her own name, and in the name of God's people, received the mission and coming of the Redeemer, with whom the initiative always remains.

Mary's role.

Mary was called to her central role, to play her unique part in her Son's work, yet her role was by no means clear to her: she 'advanced in her pilgrimage of faith, and faithfully persevered in her union with her Son unto the cross' (art. 58). She was one who lived by faith, one who entered with faith and love into the saving work of Christ. What is true of her remains true, though in a lesser degree, of the rest of redeemed mankind. It is by entering, like her, into the faith and love of Christ, that we are redeemed.

There is particular significance in the fact that Mary should have figured in the preparation for Pentecost: her association with the Holy Spirit made her place in the birth of the Church especially fitting. And at Pentecost the Spirit, who had made God's Son man in Mary, filled the Church with the life of Christ. It is not by chance that the apostles waited, in prayer, 'together with Mary the mother of Jesus' (Acts 1:14). Present at the beginning, she remains a presage of the end; for, in Mary taken up into heavenly glory, the church sees, anticipated, its own consummation. 'She was taken up body and soul into heavenly glory, when her earthly life was over, and exalted by the Lord as Queen over all things, that she might be the more fully conformed to her Son, the Lord of Lords (Rev. 19:16) and conqueror of sin and death' (art. 59).

Mary and the Church.

The relationship of Mary to the Church is twofold: she is the spiritual mother of all Christians and she is the archetype of the Church. Mariology makes sense only in relation to Christology; more simply, Mary's role in the Church stands squarely on the unique mediation of Christ. Christ our Lord is the center and meaning of our religion. He is the end of all our striving – this God who became Man and suffered and died for us, this Jesus who has loved us and who loves us with infinite love. *Lumen Gentium* firmly asserts: 'There is but one mediator: "for there is but one God and one mediator of God and men, the man Christ Jesus, who gave himself a redemption for all" (1 Tim. 2:5-6). But Mary's function as mother of men in no way obscures or diminishes this unique mediation of Christ, but rather shows its power... It flows forth from the superabundance of the merits of Christ, rests on his mediation, depends entirely on it and draws all its power from it. It does not hinder in any way the immediate union of the faithful with Christ but on the contrary fosters it' (art. 60). Mary's spiritual motherhood, her mediation, comes about because she, in virtue of the grace that she, the first of the redeemed, received from Christ has become, in turn, a source of salvation for her children.

Mary's spiritual motherhood is a reality here and now. In this respect, too, she reflects the abiding presence of her Son. Jesus Christ, our High Priest, stands before God, interceding on our behalf (cf Heb. 7:25). Similarly,

Mary's share in the redemptive work of Christ continues in her intercession before God. Because she was connected with Christ and his work on earth she, now in heaven, is able to act as intercessor for men. For the sake of the other brothers and sisters of her Son she has been raised to share in the ongoing saving import of Christ's work. 'By her maternal charity, she cares for the brethren of her Son, who still journey on earth surrounded by dangers and difficulties, until they are led into their blessed home' (art. 62).

A tradition going back at least to Saint Ambrose, holds that Mary is the archetype of the Church. She is that in the twofold mystery of her virgin motherhood. She is type of the Church 'in the order of faith, charity, and perfect union with Christ' (art. 63). Mary stands before the Church as the image in which the Church can look upon its own future perfection. Historically, that image of Mary has not been very observable in a Church which too often has borne another image, not reflective of the graciousness of Mary nor of the 'meekness and gentleness of Christ' (1 Cor. 10:1). Christians here on earth still have to battle with sin; Mary is the pattern of virtue which they will strive to imitate. But they will be transformed in the end not into her likeness but into the likeness of Christ.

One can theorize and theologize about the place of Mary in the Church and in christian life. The reality is something much more personal. We need her womanly graciousness. She can help us to cut through the unhappy history of ecclesiastical male dominance and speak to the finer feelings of men. The Church will truly be the Church of Christ when reverence for Mary is reflected in our practical regard for the daughters of Mary.

Our Mother.

With its Scripture-oriented outlook, the Second Vatican Council, has firmly expressed the place of Mary in God's saving plan: as Mother of the Messiah she is caught up into the work of her Son. It is not enough for us to admire our Lady, or to praise God for her privileges. She is our Mother who can lead us to Jesus, who will lead us to him — if we let her. Devotion to her is not something we can take up or not as we choose; she is too intimately linked to the saving plan of God. As Mother of God she is so close to Christ that we cannot ignore her without the risk of ignoring him, of forgetting him.

As Christians, we should be docile to the Holy Spirit who dwells within us. As Christians we must clothe ourselves with Christ, we must become like him in every way. The Mother of God, our mother, will help us, will enable us, to listen for the voice of the Holy Spirit, and then obey him; she will form us into the image of her Son. As her children we should, lovingly and confidently, put ourselves in her hands. Her one desire — the desire o her God and ours — is that we may become true images of her Son (cf Rom. 8:29).

SELECT BIBLIOGRAPHY

SELECT BIBLIOGRAPHY.

J. B. BAUER (ed.), *Encyclopedia of Biblical Theology*, 3 vols. (N.Y.: Sheed & Ward — 1970).

P. BENOIT, *The Passion and Resurrection of Jesus Christ* (London: Darton, Longman & Todd — 1969).

R. E. BROWN, *The Gospel According to St John*, 2 vols. (Garden City, N.Y.: Doubleday — 1966, 1970).

........................., *The Virginal Conception and Bodily Resurrection of Jesus* (N.Y.: Paulist Press — 1973).

........................., 'Luke's Description of the Virginal Conception', *Theological Studies* 35 (1974), 360-362.

C. H. DODD, *The Interpretation of the Fourth Gospel* (N.Y.: C.U.P. — 1965).

........................., *The Founder of Christianity* (London: Collins — 1971).

J. A. FITZMYER, 'The Virginal Conception of Jesus in the New Testament' *Theological Studies*, 34 (1973), 541-575.

H. GRAEF, 'Our Lady and the Church', *Vatican II on the Church*, A. Flannery, ed. (Dublin: Scepter — 1966), 136-144.

W. J. HARRINGTON, *The Gospel According to St. Luke* (Westminster: Newman — 1967).

..................................., *Christ and Life* (Chicago: Franciscan Herald Press — 1975).

J. JEREMIAS, *New Testament Theology I*. The Proclamation of Jesus (London: SCM — 1971).

X. LÉON-DUFOUR, *Resurrection and the Message of Easter* (London: Chapman — 1974).

................................, (ed.), *Dictionary of Biblical Theology* (N.Y.: Desclee — 1973).

P. LIVERMORE, 'Reflections on the Resurrection' *Scripture in Church* No. 10 — 1973. 452-460.

G. MEATH, *Scripture Rosary* (London: Catholic Truth Society — 1974).

J. B. METZ, 'Messianische Geschichte als Leidensgeschichte. Meditation zu Mk. 8:31-38', *Neues Testament und Kirche*, J. Gnilka, ed. (Freiburg-Basel-Wien: Herder — 1974), 63-70.

G. O'COLLINS, *The Resurrection of Jesus Christ* (Valley Forge, Pa.: Judson — 1973).

K. RAHNER and H. VORGRIMLER, *Concise Theological Dictionary* (London: Burns & Oates — 1965).

O. SEMMELROTH, *Commentary on the Documents of Vatican II*, H. Vorgrimler, ed. (N.Y.: Herder & Herder — 1967), 285-296.